BECOMING
WHOLEHEARTED

BECOMING WHOLEHEARTED

A Path to Who You Were Created to Be Through Connection with God, Yourself, and Others

by

ANISA SUMLAR AND LARRY BOLDEN

WELLSPRING PRESS

Becoming Wholehearted: A Path to Who You Were Created to Be Through Connection with God, Yourself, and Others

Copyright © 2025 Wellspring Group

All rights reserved. No portion of this book may be reproduced, stored in a retrieval system, distributed, or transmitted in any form or by any means—electronic, mechanical, photocopy, recording, scanning, or other—except for brief quotations in printed reviews, without the prior written permission from Wellspring Group.

Unless otherwise noted, Scripture quotations are taken from the Holy Bible, New International Version®, NIV® Copyright ©1973, 1978, 1984, 2011 by Biblica, Inc.® Used by permission. All rights reserved worldwide.

Scripture quotations marked ESV are taken from the ESV® Bible (The Holy Bible, English Standard Version®), © 2001 by Crossway, a publishing ministry of Good News Publishers. ESV Text Edition: 2025.

Scripture quotations marked CSB are taken from The Christian Standard Bible. Copyright © 2017 by Holman Bible Publishers. Used by permission. Christian Standard Bible®, and CSB® are federally registered trademarks of Holman Bible Publishers. All rights reserved.

Scripture quotations marked NASB are taken from New American Standard Bible®, Copyright © 1960, 1971, 1977, 1995, 2020 by The Lockman Foundation. All rights reserved.

Scripture quotations marked NLT are taken from *Holy Bible*, New Living Translation, copyright © 1996, 2004, 2015 by Tyndale House Foundation. Used by permission of Tyndale House Publishers, Inc., Carol Stream, Illinois 60188. All rights reserved.

Cover design: Micah Kandros
Interior design: Greg Jackson

Published in Newville, AL, by Wellspring Press, a division of Wellspring Group. Wellspring Press titles may be purchased in bulk for educational, business, fundraising, or sales promotional use. For information, please email info@wellspringgroup.org

Becomingwholehearted.org

ISBN 979-8-9935463-0-8
Library of Congress Control Number: 2025926429

Printed in the United States of America

For more than twenty years, my ministry and congregation have been reshaped by God's call to wholehearted living. I have watched weary hearts awaken, leaders emerge, and marriages heal as we embraced the biblical truth and grace of becoming wholehearted. Many believers exhaust themselves searching for a grand purpose in the larger story, but Larry and Anisa remind us that our deepest calling is to cooperate with the Triune God as He forms us into who He created, redeemed, and is restoring us to be. This book is a life-giving invitation to that journey.

—Bob Flayhart, D.Min., Founding Pastor, Oak Mountain Presbyterian Church (PCA), involved since 2009.*

Becoming Wholehearted isn't just a book; it's an encounter. As I turned each page, it felt like sitting with trusted friends who reminded me that God still meets us in the middle of our lives. Larry and Anisa write with such honesty and warmth that truth feels personal again. Their words and stories stirred something deep in me, a longing to live with an open heart as a woman, wife, mother, friend, and pastor. This book doesn't just inspire; it heals, restores, and awakens hope you may have thought was lost.

—Bobbi Lassiter, Discipleship Pastor, Covenant Methodist Church (GMC), involved since 2024

Growing up as a minority in the American South and wed into a multicultural marriage while serving pastorally in a multiethnic church has proven to be a hard yet holy journey of discovering my God-given purpose, rooted in my identity as the Beloved. The Wellspring path has given me a sound and solid footing for that journey. I am imperfectly, yet continually, risking vulnerability wherever I am and engaging more fearlessly and unashamedly. Living from being enjoyed and beloved is transcendently human, and as Larry and Anisa write, "That's as good as it gets."

—Ash Bolden, Elder and Generations Pastor, GateCity Church, non-denominational, involved since 2021

Discovering how to live from my whole heart in community has shaped every facet of my life. I am a better husband, father, son, mentor, and business leader because I have discovered the deep desires God placed within me and the fullness of His love that fills those desires. *Becoming Wholehearted* is a gracious invitation to all who long for deeper connection with their own heart, with God, and with others.

—Rob Consoli, Chief Revenue Officer of global high-tech companies, involved since 2015

*When each person began Wellspring Group's Battle for Your Heart experience.

The path to becoming wholehearted has profoundly shaped our church. Our people are experiencing the love of God and finding freedom from lies about their identity and long-held shame. As our people are discovering how to live from a place of being loved, we have experienced greater healing and unity across differences of race, culture, economic background, gender, and education. Our shared sense of purpose and fellowship has deepened, strengthening us as a diverse church living in wholehearted community and seeking to reach our diverse city.

—Will Reinmuth, Lead Pastor, All Souls Community Church (CMA), involved since 2022

Becoming Wholehearted invites us to move beyond settling or striving and into a life rooted in being fully known and fully loved by God. With honesty and wisdom, Anisa and Larry guide us from merely knowing about God's love to truly experiencing it. God has used Wellspring Group to transform my marriage, parenting, and relationships over many years, and this book captures the essence of that journey into secure, wholehearted living.

—Stephanie Shackelford, EdD., Senior Fellow at Barna Group, involved since 2020

Going on the journey to becoming wholehearted has deepened my desire, confidence, and capacity to engage others with vulnerability and grace. As I have grown in living more connected to my heart, God's heart, and the hearts of others, my relationships with my wife, other men, and my work colleagues have been transformed. As a result, I am now experiencing a depth of connection throughout my relationships I once believed was impossible—the growing freedom, joy, and peace that flows from increasingly becoming who God created me to be.

—David Wilson, attorney, former public company General Counsel, involved since 2018

Becoming Wholehearted gives language to the inner battle we all feel and offers a grace-filled path toward real and lasting transformation. Larry and Anisa write with honesty, humility, and a lived-in theology that awakens hope. If you're longing for deeper intimacy with God, healing for the divided places in your heart, or a community where grace actually forms people, this book will help you take the next step.

—Ryan Johnson, D.Min., Pastor, New City Church (PCA), involved since 2022

Dedication

From Larry

To my parents, Paul and Rosalyn Bolden, who gave me life, a good name, and loved me to the best of their capacity. I pray that as you are now in the great cloud of witnesses you will see in some way the eternal fruit of your lives.

To my wife, Mary, and son, Jonathan, who have borne the greatest cost of my walking in pride, which sabotaged my becoming a wholehearted husband and father earlier in life. I am forever grateful for your loving forgiveness, perseverance, and belief that, in humility, I can become who I long to be as a husband and a father. To Laurie, our beloved daughter-in-law, who courageously and humbly chose to restore your marriage and our family.

To Elise, Audrey, Elliott, Ann Catherine, and Darcy—my beloved grandchildren. Thank you for being part of my journey to discover the playfulness of being a wholehearted granddaddy. I look forward to the years to come on my "final glide path."

From Anisa

To my family who has taught me what it is to love and be loved unconditionally. A special thank you to my husband, JJ, for allowing me to share some of the still raw places in our story because you have a deep and abiding belief in me and God's call on me as a woman and writer.

From Larry and Anisa

To our Wellspring Group community—the men and women who have walked with us for more than two decades along the path to becoming wholehearted.

Finally, to all the people who nodded and looked as if they believed us when we said we will finish this book.

Contents

Foreword 11
Introduction 13

Part 1: The Way of Pride

Chapter 1: Encountering God in a Coffee Shop
    Discovering fullness of life in community 21
Chapter 2: From Eden to a Dorm Room
    The longing for restored connection. 33
Chapter 3: Sculptures & Self-Protective Strategies
    The always present battle for glory 47

Part 2: Overcoming Obstacles to Connection

Chapter 4: Colorful Socks
    What choices reveal about the true state of your heart. . . 65
Chapter 5: Demolishing Dams
    Beliefs that block connection 81
Chapter 6: I Will Come to You
    Connecting to the God who loves and likes you 95
Chapter 7: I Will Come to You in Community
    Opening your heart to love and be loved
    in community 109
Chapter 8: Desires That Deceive
    How desires can sabotage what we long for 123

Part 3: The Way of Humility

Chapter 9: Is There Another Way?
    How the Father prepares his son for the cross 141
Chapter 10: Tell Me I'm a Good Man
    Moving from "earn this" to "receive this" 156

Chapter 11: No Pain Wasted
      Broken down break through 169
Chapter 12: God Doesn't Set You Up for Failure
      Embracing repentance and mourning to become
      who you're created to be 181
Chapter 13: Dare to Risk
      Becoming who you are created to be, together 195

Next Steps. 205
Acknowledgments 207
Glossary. 209

Tools

Desires Chart 214
Deepest Desires 215
Feelings Chart 216
The Elevator Model of the Heart 218
State of the Heart. 219
Four Levels Scripture Templates 220
Notes 221

Foreword

In 1967, I was a young fighter pilot flying combat missions in Vietnam when I was shot down, captured, and imprisoned for five years. In the harsh prison cells of the "Hanoi Hilton," I learned the significance of love and connection when it comes to survival. Like most of the long-term prisoners, I spent hours each day in prayer. This gave me comfort and confidence in God's love despite my circumstances. Later, when we were moved to larger cells, we established a community where we experienced God's love expressed through human connection—gaining optimism about the future and courage to hold on.

Returning home, I built a family and a career, with faith always part of my life. I attended church and read Scripture regularly, and I wasn't aware that anything was missing. But in 2004, I met Larry Bolden, who invited me to a Battle for the Heart retreat. There, I discovered how much more God had for me.

The Battle for the Heart introduced me to living from my whole heart and opening my heart more fully to God's love. During the first morning's session, after a one-hour teaching, we spent an hour in silence and solitude. In my room, I turned off the lights and sat in darkness. As I opened my heart, I experienced God's love deeper than I ever had before. I felt immense joy as tears rolled down my face. I realized that God had been showing me his love every day, but I had not been receiving it.

As I began consistently connecting with God's love, I grew in confidence and security—and it changed everything. My walk with God deepened. My marriage grew stronger as I was able to love my wife, Mary, in ways that made her feel valued and secure. My relationships with others became more unconditional. And my work in leadership training shifted toward helping others lead with humility and confidence in God's love, showing them how acts of love build trust and confidence in those they serve.

Now, looking back at 82, if asked what I believe is the most critical element of a healthy, happy life, of leadership that inspires loyalty, and of fulfilling God's command to love others, it would be this: personal security that comes from deep confidence in God's love.

That is why I can say *Becoming Wholehearted* is one of the most important books I have ever read. For many years, Mary and I have had life-changing experiences at the retreats that are the foundation of the stories and teachings in this book. In *Becoming Wholehearted*, you will learn to open your heart to God's love in ways that bring lasting change—and to love others in ways that change them.

When I first met Larry, I could not have imagined how much he would impact my life. In the years since, and through knowing Anisa as well, I have been deeply inspired by the way they live—confident in and surrendered to God's love, leading with humility, and inviting others into deeper experiences of God's heart.

Make this book one you read again and again. The more you open your heart to receive God's love, the more you will become the person God created you to be.

Lee Ellis, Vietnam POW veteran, author of the book, *Leading with Honor—Leadership Lessons from the Hanoi Hilton*, leadership speaker and a consultant/coach for the United States military and major corporations.

Introduction

Anisa

I sat beside a window, light streaming in, clutching my Bible close, and praying with everything I had in my desperately seeking thirteen-year-old heart.

God, if you're real, I need you to speak to me.

With decades between then and now, I can't recall what drove my desperation. But I remember feeling my life was over, ruined beyond repair. Looking back, it wasn't anything major. Nothing shocking or truly dangerous ever pierced the protective bubble of my childhood. At that age, though, without the perspective maturity brings, whatever it was felt truly disastrous. So, I prayed the prayer, the only one I knew to offer.

I'm going to open my Bible, and whatever verse I put my finger on, that's what I'm going to believe you're speaking to me.

With maturity I realize that's not a wise way to pray, but I believe that day God saw the naïve heart of a child longing to hear him, to receive his comfort. Out of his love and grace, he reached down from heaven to tenderly whisper these words:

> I, the Lord, have called you in righteousness; I will take hold of your hand. I will keep you and will make you to be a covenant for the people and a light for the Gentiles, to open eyes that are blind, to free captives from prison and to release from the dungeon those who sit in darkness. (Isaiah 42:6–7)

That experience became, for me, life-altering—an ordinary moment taking on extraordinary importance—as God met me in a deeply personal way. Full of childlike innocence and wonder, it was a first step in coming to know God as trustworthy and longing for a relationship with me. I gained a vision of who he created me to be—someone who would walk closely with him, hand in hand, partnering with him in setting captives free. I felt seen, known, valued, and trusted, which gave me a sense of purpose and significance. For the first time, I realized I was created for something bigger than the small story consuming me. I glimpsed a Larger Story that I could give my life to.

But that invitation God whispered to a young girl isn't just for me. He comes to you, inviting you into a deeply intimate, personal relationship with him in the grand adventure of his Larger Story. In this Story you can discover the answers to your deepest heart questions—questions such as "Am I loved?," "Who am I?," and "Why am I here?" This place of intimate connection is the path to becoming who God created you to be and experiencing the fullness of life we all long for.

But few of us consistently experience that fullness. Why is that?

In my story, in the ensuing years, much of my childlike wonder and trust faded. Life happened. Disappointments rolled in as cresting waves one after another. In the swirling undertow of my own small story, I lost sight of the captivating vision of God's Larger Story.

Gradually, I began shutting down parts of my heart, not sure what to do with my pain and unanswered questions. Maybe you've been there. Or maybe you never held wonder and trust to begin with, your negative experience of life or people entrusted with your child's heart having tainted your view of a God who is good.

One thing I discovered, though, in the ebbs and flows of my relationship with God is that he never gives up on pursuing my heart. Though I didn't recognize it as such at the time, one example of his pursuit came at the close of 2004 through my coauthor Larry offering me a very part time job joining him in a year-old ministry called Wellspring Group. Larry and a small group of men had begun developing retreats called Battle for the Heart.

Building from a foundation of Proverbs 4:23, they sought to live and equip others to live from their whole hearts so that God's love and life could flow more freely to and through the "wellspring" of their hearts.

This concept of living from a whole heart was challenging to me. When I would join these men and their wives after retreats to celebrate what God had done, it seemed like entering a different world. The men would share their feelings and ask one another questions related to how God was meeting their deepest desires. My logic-oriented brain didn't know what to do with people who related to one another on that level. It felt like they all had a playbook I hadn't been given. And honestly, I didn't care to read it. I lived in the practical and the efficient, and nothing about what I was experiencing seemed to fit.

Then, in 2008, when we expanded Battle for the Heart to an almost yearlong spiritual formation process open also to women, God opened my eyes to what it means to become wholehearted. I began to see the impact of years of gradually shutting down parts of my heart. God created my heart to desire, feel, think, and choose. When I unknowingly shut down parts of my heart, I wasn't allowing God's love to touch those fearful, self-protected places. To become who I was created to be, I had to open my whole heart to experience God's love, the only power strong enough to bring lasting life transformation.

So, back to my question: Why aren't more of us consistently experiencing the fullness of life we long for? Why do we struggle to grow in Christlike character? The answer doesn't lie in doing more. It lies in becoming more, becoming wholehearted. Change happens when we move from knowledge about God's love to deep, wholehearted knowing of God's love. This means you not only *think* you are loved by God, you *feel* loved; you experience God's love that satisfies your *deepest desires* to be seen, known, and valued; and you begin to make *choices* out of trust in God's love and goodness rather than fear.

What does that look like? Part of my journey to becoming wholehearted has been rediscovering my passion for writing. When Larry invited me to join him as coauthor of this book, I questioned whether I was willing to embrace the vulnerability of opening the broken parts of my story to people who do not know me, who may even judge and reject me. In the midst of those fears, I went back to that moment when, as a young girl God gave me a vision of who he created me to be—his partner in setting the captives free. I knew that if just one person gained increasing freedom through this book, I needed to take the risk and step into my part in God's Larger Story. But to take that step I had to trust that God loves me and his heart toward me is good. However this book is received, God sees me. He still knows me. He still holds my hand as he guides me into his purposes for my life. So, I, along with Larry, offer these stories and truths God has entrusted to us in a spirit of humility, praying that you, like us, are on a path to the freedom of being who God created us to be.

This book is for those who wonder, like Paul, why they do the things they do and not the things they want to do (see Romans 7:15–20). It is for those who want to move from knowledge about God's love to a wholehearted knowing of his love. It is the experience of God's love in our whole hearts that closes the disconnect between the rational, biblical truth we know and try to live from and the truth we react from under pressure. This happens as we live increasingly connected to our own hearts, to God's heart, and the hearts of others. It is living in the reality of Ephesians 3:16–19:

> I pray that out of his glorious riches he may strengthen you with power through his Spirit in your inner being, so that Christ may dwell in your hearts through faith. And I pray that you, being rooted and established in love, may have power, together with all the Lord's holy people, to grasp how wide and long and high and deep is the love of Christ, and to know this love that surpasses knowledge—that you may be filled to the measure of all the fullness of God.

For more than twenty years we have seen thousands move from surface-level connections with God and others to vibrant relationships that contribute to personal and spiritual growth; pastors truly believing for the first time that God loves and even likes them; marriages restored; business leaders changing from distant and reserved to more caring and compassionate leaders focused not only on the good of the business but also on creating an environment where people flourish.

In *Becoming Wholehearted*, we've taken key concepts and biblical truths from more than two decades of ministry and illustrated them through our own stories and those of our alumni. This book is rooted in scripture that is being lived out in real lives that are still unfolding. You will not relate to every story. You may not even find any stories that match your life experience. But our hope is that you will find yourself in the shared longing for deep, authentic connection and for a life of purpose that flows out of knowing your true identity in Christ.

Becoming Wholehearted has been in the making several years. Even as we were writing, God was deepening in us truth about his love for each of us, challenging our distortions and self-protective strategies, and inviting us into deeper levels of humility. We invite you to join us on this path to becoming the person God has created you to be—knowing his love, confidently living in your identity as a beloved image bearer, and fulfilling your purpose wherever God has placed you.

PART 1

The Way of Pride

How we became disconnected from our own hearts, God, and others

CHAPTER 1

Encountering God in a Coffee Shop

Discovering fullness of life in community

Larry

Have you ever looked at your life and longed for something more? Or found yourself asking hard questions about life, yourself, and God?

That's where I found myself in the spring of 2003. On my fiftieth birthday I had a wonderful evening with friends and family, followed by a meaningful surprise party the next day with the youth from church. I felt loved, celebrated, and grateful. I looked back on over thirty-five years of walking with the Lord, including thirteen years in business and thirteen in pastoral ministry, with satisfaction. Yet I also felt deep weariness.

The prior years had held beautiful moments of deep connection with God and others, but also significant pain as relationships I once thought solid became fractured. Through that, I had begun to see the cost of my relentless desire to achieve—costs to those I loved, to God, and to myself.

In 2002, through scripture, prayer, and discernment with trusted friends, God had surprised my wife, Mary, and me by clearly guiding us out of pastoral ministry. We were peaceful about this. The challenge was God didn't tell us what was next! Now, turning fifty and on sabbatical, I was at a crossroads where I found myself asking God, "Who am I, who have you uniquely created me to be, and what do you want me to do?" Deep questions with no easy answers.

I don't know where you are on your journey, but if you've picked up this book, chances are you find yourself at a crossroads or asking similar questions or searching for that almost indefinable something "more." Maybe you're diving into the adventures of young adulthood and trying to figure out where you belong.

Or perhaps you're trying to survive the chaotic messiness of the middle adult years, facing disappointment because life isn't turning out how you'd envisioned. In the disappointment maybe you struggle to reconcile the familiar truths of scripture with your actual experience of God, life, and relationships.

Maybe you've passed both those seasons and you're reflecting from the slower paced, supposed-to-be golden years, questioning whether you have anything else to offer.

Whatever stage of life you find yourself in, young or old, married or single, well off financially or just barely scraping by, this book is for you. How can I say that with such confidence? Because you are a human being and we are more alike than different. Under all the outward trappings, human beings have the same deep desires—such as belonging, adventure, beauty, justice, freedom, love, identity, and purpose. Desires connected to the questions we're all asking about God, life, ourselves, and others. All these desires and all these questions originate from the same source: the heart.

This book is about understanding and connecting to your heart—the desiring, feeling, thinking, choosing part of you—and then deeply connecting with God and others. This is what we call living wholeheartedly.

Becoming wholehearted is life changing because it is in the intersection with our heart, God's heart, and the hearts of others that we authentically experience God's presence transforming us into the person God created us to be, bringing the fullness of life we long for.

Becoming wholehearted isn't easy and doesn't happen overnight. But in this book, we share a proven, biblical path that, if followed, will propel you on a life-long journey of increasingly experiencing deep, authentic, life-giving heart connections that lead to lasting change. This wholehearted experience of life is what I was missing at that milestone birthday more than two decades ago. Yet God had already been preparing me to discover this ancient path that David called

Figure 1.0

Wholehearted

Living increasingly connected to your heart, God's heart, and the hearts of others

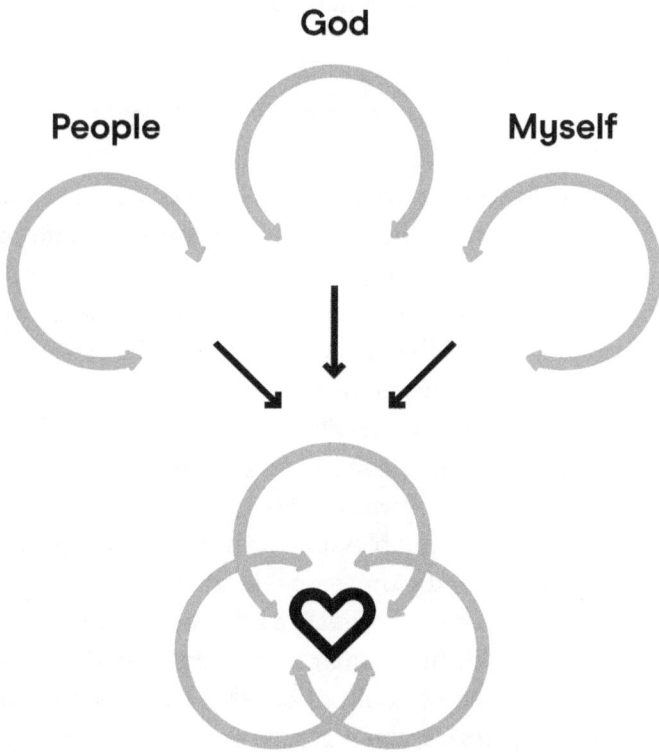

"the everlasting way" (Psalm 139:24 NASB). For several years, I consistently meditated on David's prayer in Psalm 139 and consistently heard the Holy Spirit whispering to me, "I know you. In the darkness I see you. No matter where you are or where you go, my right hand holds you fast. You are mine, fearfully and wonderfully made." In all the uncertainties, I sensed God calling me to simply trust his loving presence and goodness.

So now, in this time of sabbatical, God led me to the North Georgia Mountains for twelve days of prayer and fasting. In the pain and the blessing of the past and uncertainty of the future, I longed to rest, recover, and most of all simply to be with God in the solitude and the silence of nature. I knew deep down there was more he had for me than what I'd yet experienced, and I wanted to find out what it was.

A Vision Birthed

As I beheld God's glory in the stillness of nature, I spent long times in prayer and listening to him in the scriptures and through books. I felt his presence and love surround me, empowering me to risk praying that God would search my heart. I asked him to reveal the anxious thoughts that drove me, the pain I'd caused others, and the pain others had caused me (Psalm 139:23–24, NASB).

As he did, I grieved, repented, and experienced his overwhelming love and forgiveness. I increasingly saw how God had always been working in my life, even in how he created me, how he crafted my life through pain and blessings as his hand held me and guided me. Then, I began to dream again—to glimpse his purpose for the rest of my life, which was to create a safe place where people could come to connect to his heart, their own hearts, and the hearts of others. A place where people could discover the redemptive thread of God's love in their stories, and regardless of their stories, could experience the life-giving power of belonging.

On my last day in the mountains, I went one last time to a clear, bubbling stream in the woods where God had consistently met me, to simply be with him in this space, to pause, worship, and give thanks for his faithfulness. Then, as I started to leave, I looked up into what had been bare trees, to see them budding with leaves. I sensed God whisper, "Winter is past; spring has come." A new joy and hope filled my heart.

In just a few months, my joy and hope would be tested and strengthened as I experienced a glimpse of that dream through the crucible of an intense graduate school program in Christian counseling. In this encouraging, challenging place, God took me by the hand to plunge me into the questions I had been asking all my life, without even realizing it.

Three Essential Questions

The three questions I'd been asking in various ways all my life were profoundly simple.

Am I loved?	Speaks to our experience of **intimacy**, of being seen, known, and respected
Who am I?	Speaks to our sense of **identity**, the truth of who we are as human beings
Why am I here?	Speaks to our **purpose**, the reason we exist

We all, in some way, are asking these questions because they flow out of God's desires for our lives. God designed us to answer these questions in the context of relational connection. In other words, through becoming wholehearted human beings.

Becoming Wholehearted: A Life of Flourishing

Why does becoming wholehearted matter? Because we are relational beings, created in the image of a relational God. God created us out of love, to be loved, so that we can love. He *made* us for connection—deep, meaningful, intimate connection where people see his image in us and, in response, inspire us to become all he created us to be. In connections we are given courage when we feel like giving up, celebrated when we succeed, comforted when we grieve, and challenged when we fall short of being the person who God created us to be—the person we long to be. "Alone" becomes a place we occasionally withdraw to, not a state of being.

Because we are relational beings, we cannot flourish apart from relationship with the God in whose image we were created. We cannot truly be the father, mother, sister, brother, husband, wife, or friend God calls us to be apart from intimate connections with him and with other people, the kinds of connections where we see and know others and are seen and known by them.

In 2022 Robert Waldinger, MD, and Marc Schulz, PhD, published a book chronicling a Harvard longevity study on happiness. The study tracked a group of 724 teens and young adults through their entire lifespan and continues with more than thirteen hundred of their descendants. In *The Good Life: Lessons from the World's Longest Scientific Study of Happiness*, they bottom line their findings:

> Good relationships are significant enough that if we had to take all eighty-four years of the Harvard study and boil it down to a single principle for living, one life investment that is supported by similar findings across a wide variety of other studies, it would be this: Good relationships keep us healthier and happier. Period.[1]

God created us to thrive in relationships. Research simply affirms the goodness of God's design.

Still, despite our desires for intimate connection and the critical role of such relationships to our mental, emotional, and physical health, many of us live isolated. Our fast-paced, technology-driven lifestyles make it difficult to build authentic, life-giving relationships. The relationships we are created for, that contribute to our overall sense of well-being, are those in which we experience frequent, positive, and satisfying interactions with people we can rely on.

Jesus modeled this type of relationship as he sacrificially gave himself to his disciples. He then called his followers to "love one another as I have loved you" (see John 13:1–17; 34–35). This is biblical community.

Through those twelve days in the mountains in spring 2003, then my graduate school summer intensive, and through a small group of men during that fall, God kept opening this vision of community to Mary and me in multiple ways. I will never forget the Holy Spirit's invitation into a risky, scary leap of faith to build a place, a space called Wellspring Group, to see this vision become reality. With trepidation and trembling faith, we leapt.

Since then, God has been drawing us into a deepening, challenging, painfully beautiful, transformational experience of discovering how to effectively build the type of community Jesus prayed for in John 17:20–26 and Paul envisioned in Ephesians 3:14–4:16.

My coauthor, Anisa, and I have walked in this type of community alongside thousands of men and women who have been part of Wellspring Group and gone through the Battle for the Heart—a path that inspires and equips people with the heart and skills of biblical, wholehearted community. Along the way, as you will see throughout this book, our own lives and relationships continue to be transformed.

There, in the safety of relationships in which we are seen, known, and respected, we are slowly opening our hearts to risk being loved by Christ through other believers. We are discovering our whole hearts—even the hidden, shut-down places of pain, fear, and unbelief. We are discovering and repenting of how we have been taking our questions to people and experiences instead of to the God who created us. Then in community we are experiencing the love "that transcends knowledge" permeating the depths of our hearts so that increasingly we act and react out of who God created us to be and Christ redeemed us to be. We are experiencing the goodness of God in community.

As you reflect on your life, how have you experienced community like this—community where you are free to be yourself? Where you'll find acceptance wherever you are on the path, but also, in God's time and way, be challenged to go deeper into who God created you to be?

Your experience may have been like mine where you've questioned if this type of community is even possible. There have been many times when I've cried out to God and said it's just too hard, I want to give up. But then the Holy Spirit kept gently asking me, "Is the gospel true?" Deep within, I know that the good news of the Father's love for me and for you is true. Out of love, he sent Jesus, "the way the truth and life" (John 14:6) to lead us home to the Father and empower us to love one another as he loves us.

This is wholehearted community—where we experience a depth of connection that, through the Holy Spirit, transcends mere human conversation and invites us into an ongoing encounter with the divine presence, the very glory of God. In this place, God answers the questions of our hearts and leads us into fullness of life and the "more" we all long for. For over twenty years, he has been doing this in different ways and different spaces, including coffee shops . . .

Coffee Shop Connections

Several years ago, in the cold, wintry predawn hours I met two longtime friends at a neighborhood coffee shop. Outside, the wind cut through the dark morning, a chilling echo of the storm inside me. My heart felt heavy, weighed down by fear and doubt. Two days earlier, I had been blindsided by a crisis involving people I loved. I won't go into details, but it was a crisis that touched our organization, sparking deep fears that I'd not yet identified.

After we placed our order, we sat down. Bryan and Rob are accomplished business leaders as well as members of Wellspring Group's board. They share a similar desire to wholeheartedly love

God and others in every area of their lives. We meet regularly for mutual connection, so after we finished a few minutes of casual conversation, one of them suggested we share how we were coming into the meeting. I immediately teared up.

As they asked about the tears, I realized their presence gave me strength. I knew at a gut level these were good, godly men—men who loved me. The strength of their love gave me courage to pause, let go, and trust I was not alone. I was safe.

As they asked a few simple questions, I shared briefly about what was going on inside me. Then Rob asked a profound question, one that challenged me to look beyond the current circumstances.

"What is at stake in how you respond in this situation?"

I paused for what seemed like a long time. As they patiently waited, I could feel the fear: what if everything we've built falls apart? I've failed to come through. What will people think?

Then the fears began to recede as I touched something deeper—something God had been building into the depths of my heart for over twenty years. It was something these men deeply believed. Something simple.

What was at stake in my response? Whether or not I would be the man God created me to be, a man who engages this challenge with strength and love regardless of the outcomes.

As I tearfully shared that response, Bryan leaned in with tears in his own eyes and spoke directly to my open, trusting heart, "Larry it's about the people, not the organization. God cares more about the people than the structure."

That conviction didn't come easily for a high achieving, outcomes-oriented leader like Bryan. That conviction came out of the fires of our lives, out of the truth we had experienced over twenty years together. Those words now pierced my heart, giving me courage to take a leap of faith.

Yes, I will let go of the fears. I will engage the situation, the people, with strength and love regardless of the outcomes.

In that moment, I knew these men I trusted, who had authority in my life, believed in God and me. They believed that regardless of the potential negative outcomes, God's love would be enough to sustain us. And whatever the fallout might be, we would face it together.

Their response spoke directly to my three heart questions.

1. **Am I loved?** Yes. I experienced being known, respected, safe, and loved.
2. **Who am I?** Knowing I'm loved gave me confidence to believe that I am who God created me to be—a man and leader deeply loved by God and dependent upon him.
3. **Why am I here?** The answers to my first two questions gave me courage to engage the situation with the strength and love of Christ.

In a neighborhood coffee shop, as the three of us risked sharing our open, broken, vulnerable hearts, we encountered the presence of Christ. His love, grace, and truth touched the fears and unbelief deep within my heart, setting me free to be loved and to love. I experienced what Dr. David Benner, a psychologist and spiritual director, states in his book *Surrender to Love*:

> Genuine transformation requires vulnerability. It is not the fact of being loved unconditionally that is life-changing. It is the risky experience of *allowing myself* to be loved unconditionally.[2]

Until we know we are loved and safe, we will not fully open our hearts to the sacrificial, transforming love of Christ. The gospel simply bounces off the hard soil of the fearful, shut-down parts of our hearts.

As the light of day broke through the darkness outside the coffee shop, we knew we had experienced the transforming light and love of Christ filling our hearts for his glory and our deep satisfaction and fulfillment.

Our Invitation to You

It is this experience of Christ's love filling *your* heart within community that Anisa and I invite you to explore as we journey together in the following pages. In our time together, you will discover what it means to live from your whole heart—integrating your desires, feelings, thoughts, and choices—and how that gives you the capacity to more fully know yourself, to more fully connect to God and others, and to build wholehearted community. Wholehearted community is, at its core, a journey into personally and together knowing the love of Christ that transcends knowledge so that we may be filled with the fullness of God (see Ephesians 3:14–19).

To do this, we have broken this book into three parts to guide our time and have a helpful path to follow.

Part 1 explores the costs when we live from the Way of Pride. We walk in pride when we consciously or unconsciously choose independence. We will see how pride keeps us from experiencing God's love in the depths of our hearts and how, in pride, we turn to ourselves, to people, and to experiences to answer our deepest questions. This keeps us from truly knowing ourselves and experiencing the fullness of life we long for.

Part 2 explores overcoming the obstacles that prevent connection with ourselves, with God, and with others. We saw what intimate life-giving connection can look like in my coffee shop story with Bryan and Rob: these friends spoke into my fears, affirmed my identity as God's beloved child, and propelled me into my purpose of being the man I long to be, that God created me to be. You, too, can experience divine intimacy, identity, and purpose through connection.

Part 3 explores how we follow in Jesus' footsteps when we choose the Way of Humility. We walk in humility when we die to the Way of Pride, often through suffering, trusting God to bring resurrection, life, and glory in his time and way. The Way of Humility leads to increased connection as we vulnerably surrender to God's love and become a channel of his love to others.

As human beings, we cannot answer one another's deep-heart questions. Only God's love can validate our worth and determine our identity and purpose. But as Bryan and Rob exemplified, we as the Body of Christ are created and redeemed to be echoes of God's voice, affirming his life-giving words of love, grace, and truth to one another. Christ lived, died, and rose again to create a Body in whom his very presence, his glory, dwells and overflows; a place where we and all who are "weary and heavy laden" can bring our broken pieces, our pride-filled lives, our deepest questions. Only then can we come to know that we are seen, accepted, and loved. Through this place of "knowing" we discover who God created us to be and how he longs to reveal his very heart through us.

This is the life we long for! More than that, it is the life we are created for—becoming wholehearted, experiencing fullness of life with God. To truly understand that, though, we must go back to . . .

In the beginning . . .

FOR DEEPER CONNECTION

Personalize

How has being connected—or feeling disconnected—from God and others impacted your sense of satisfaction with your life?

Gain Awareness

What feelings are stirred as you consider the significance of relationships where you are seen, known, valued, and respected?

As you consider your current relationships with God and others who are important to you, what do you long for those to look like?

Respond

As you feel led, take a moment to share with God what you long for in your relationship with him, being honest about any fears and doubts.

CHAPTER 2

From Eden to a Dorm Room

The longing for restored connection

Anisa

Have you ever sat outside in the cool of the morning waiting for the sun to rise? In those moments when shadows cling to the trees and the darkness begins to fade there is an expectant hum. All of creation seems to hold its breath waiting for beauty to unfold on a canvas stretched end to end as far as the eye can see.

That must have been what it felt like at creation when all was dark and deep and waiting for the words to issue forth, "Let there be." The Spirit of God hovered expectantly, and what once was a void became something unimaginably glorious. Light burst forth and stars beyond counting appeared. The unveiling of beauty—God's glory—was displayed for all created beings to walk among—to smell, to breathe in deeply, to experience. Eden embodied all that was good and right and just. To look around, to enter into his creation was to experience who he was. It was to feel his love and his majesty, to see his fingerprint in the fragile flower and the magnificent towering trees, to know the Creator because everything around whispered of him.

All of creation God spoke into being—except for man and woman. When God created Adam, he drew dust from the ground, handcrafted him, and intimately placed something of his very image in him (see Genesis 1:26). Face to face, God breathed life into him (v. 2:7). God walked with him, talked with him. Then, recognizing Adam's need for companionship, God put him to sleep, withdrew a rib, and fashioned

Eve—bone of his bone, flesh of his flesh (vv. 20–23). Nothing else in all creation boasted such an intimate touch of the Creator.

In that place of majestic beauty, God walked in the cool of the day with the most glorious of all his creation, the only ones whom he crowned with his own glory: human beings created in his image. He came to them, was present with them as they explored the intricate weave of the fern's leaf, and he delighted in their delight. A relational God pursued relationship with human beings.

There is something vulnerably intimate about Eden—a Creator displaying his love for his creation—making visible that which would otherwise be invisible. Love moved out. Love overflowed. And we see in creation's story the love of the Father, the Son, and the Spirit intimately connecting, infinitely loving, overflowing.

Can you imagine walking in Eden and experiencing that loving connection with God?

It's the life we were created for—a life of intimate connection with God and others. It is in our relationships that the image of God in us is most fully realized.

In the first pages of scripture God demonstrates his intent for human beings to experience abundance and fulfillment through connection with himself and one another. In Eden, God met not only Adam and Eve's physical needs but their relational and spiritual ones, including satisfying their deepest desires, thus answering their deepest heart questions.

God met their desire for intimacy through the way he created them—with tender care that flowed from love. He met their desire for identity by creating them in his image. The core of their identity was a beloved image bearer. And from that identity flowed their purpose—to represent him, and to reveal who he is, his very character as they ruled over creation on his behalf. When we live in intimate connection with God and others, fulfilling our purpose as God's image bearers, we experience a merging of divine intimacy, identity, and purpose that glorifies God and satisfies the human heart. It is the fullness of life we long for.

Eden speaks of God's original design for humanity. By creating us in his image, he gave us the capacity to reveal his glory, the glory he revealed in the Garden through creation.

God's glory is expressed through his goodness. We see this in an interchange between Moses and God in Exodus 33:18-19:

> Then Moses said, "Now show me your glory."
> And the LORD said, "I will cause all my goodness to pass in front of you, and I will proclaim my name, the LORD, in your presence. I will have mercy on whom I will have mercy, and I will have compassion on whom I will have compassion."

In this passage, God speaks of his goodness—his internal essence—manifest as mercy and compassion. In Exodus 34:6-7 he adds that he is loving, faithful, forgiving, and just. For our purposes in this book, we use the terms *love*, *grace* (unmerited favor), and *truth* as a simple way to explain God's glory in relationship to us as human beings.

God's Desire, Evil's Desire

God's desire since creation has always been and always will be to reveal his glory on earth through human beings created in his image. This happens as we, through intimate connection with Christ, experience love that empowers us to love others. As John says, "We love because he first loved us" (1 John 4:19).

Evil's desire—that is, everything that exalts itself against God, including Satan, our unredeemed flesh, and the fallen world—has always been and always will be to disrupt intimacy so God's glory in us is diminished. This is because wherever God's glory flows, the powers of darkness recede. Evil cannot create; it can only distort. Therefore, Evil tempts us to choose independence from God which leads to disconnection and decreased capacity to reveal God's goodness.

How does Evil tempt us? It's easy to recognize obvious sins that lead to disconnection—those that are cruel, lawless, or cause pain to others. But we often miss the insidious ways Evil tempts us to choose the Way of Pride by attempting to make life work on our

Figure 2.0

God's Desire

To reveal his glory through your heart overflowing with his love, grace, and truth

Evil's Desire

To stop, diminish, or distort the life and glory of God flowing through your heart

Your Desire

What do you desire?

own terms. In independence, we miss the opportunity to discover more of God's character. When we don't know his character, we can't represent who he truly is.

Imagine you are given the honor of representing your company's president and making decisions on his or her behalf, but you rarely meet. You might memorize the company handbook, but if you only minimally understand the president's character and thoughts, how effective would you be? Despite your best intentions, ultimately, you would misrepresent them because you do not truly know them.

Similarly, Evil's plan is usually not to tempt you to something as drastic as a life of crime. It is to tempt you to walk independent of God's glory—of his love, grace, and truth—so you will misrepresent him in the small choices you make day in and day out. It is to tempt you to like and repost what you know to be divisive messages on social media. To look down on those who don't think like you, act like you, look like you. To treat the broken with judgment instead of compassion. This is how we sin. This is how we fall short of the glory of God without even realizing it. We fail to be who we are created to be.

Every act of God is loving. And he created us in his image so that every act of ours can be loving. But because God's desires and Evil's desires are opposing, we were born into an epic battle, and our hearts—the channel through which we display God's glory—is the battlefield.

What is this battle we bear witness to? It is a battle against everything "that sets itself up against the knowledge of God" (2 Corinthians 10:5). Ultimately, it is a battle for glory.

We see God's desire for his glory to be displayed in the Old Testament book of Habakkuk: "For the earth will be filled with the knowledge of the glory of the Lord as the waters cover the sea" (v. 2:14).

God longs for all created beings to know him and goes to extravagant lengths to make himself known. Through the beauty of creation we taste, feel, see, smell, and hear his glory. It is a tangible, experiential representation of an unseen Creator. But the greatest of his creations—the most wondrous display of God's glory, his goodness, kindness, compassion, and character—is you.

What about you? What do you desire? Do you long to experience the fullness of life that comes from living as God's image bearer and representing him on the earth, taking your place in a great adventure that started before you were born and will continue after you're gone? Do you long to have impact, to make a difference for good, to experience beauty through relationship or creative expression?

These desires reflect God's desires for you, his invitation to you. As you live from these God-given desires, you have opportunity to display God's glory and goodness as you are transformed by his love and offer that same transforming love to others. But, to win the battle for your heart and to increasingly display God's glory, you must first recognize the significance of the battle. This is something I first became aware of in college but only fully understood years later.

The Wellspring of Your Heart

I started college passionate about making a difference in the world. At nineteen, my love for the Lord had already led me around the globe on a couple of short-term missions. I didn't know what God had for me long-term but rooted in me was this longing to connect with my purpose, to be the person God created me to be.

Like many my age, though, I also had strong opinions regarding the direction I wanted my life to take. Dreams of independence, of a family, and career and financial success. I wanted to follow God's plan for my life, but I wanted a say in what that looked like. I feared that giving God total control of my life would mean giving up my dreams, my desires.

One afternoon I sat on the narrow bed in my dormitory scribbling a prayer I would later pin to my wall. I remember how the last line captured the internal struggle I was experiencing: God, give me an undivided heart (Psalm 86:11).

I didn't fully understand my heart at that time, but I knew enough to recognize there was a battle raging within me. Would I fully surrender my heart, my desires, to him? Or would I seek compromise, to somehow serve God without sacrificing the other things I longed for? Much like Robert Frost describes in "The Road Not Taken," I faced two diverging roads—one, the Way of Pride; the other, of Humility—and I knew deep down that which one I took would make all the difference. My heartfelt prayer was a desperate cry for God to somehow resolve my internal battle so I could choose the road that would lead to being the woman he created me to be.

Pastor Timothy Keller addressed this issue of the heart's direction in a blog titled "The Revolutionary Christian Heart." In it he said,

> The heart is used as a metaphor for the seat of our most basic orientation, our deepest commitments—what we trust the most (Proverbs 3:5; 23:26); it is what we most love and hope in, what we most treasure, what captures our imagination (Matthew 6:21). Every heart has an inclination (Genesis 6:5), something it is directed toward. The direction of the heart, then, controls everything—our thinking, feeling, decisions, and actions.[3]

The heart determines to whom and to what we give our love, our hope, and our trust. It determines the extent to which we experience intimacy, which in turn shapes our understanding of our identity and affects our capacity to fulfill our purpose. This makes the heart the control center of our lives.

In the crux of battle, when desires war within us, the question we face is which way we will direct our hearts. Will we turn to God, in trust? Or will we seek another way?

Proverbs 4:23 says about the heart: "Above all else, guard your heart, for it is the wellspring of life" (NIV 1984 edition).

It is hard to grasp, in modern times, the significance of the heart as a wellspring, a source of life-giving water. But in the ancient world people had to walk, sometimes miles, to draw water and carefully take it back home. Water sources were highly valued and effectively guarded because their availability determined life and death.

I understand more of the significance of water sources since moving to a rural area with several wooded acres set off from the road. My family relies on a well to meet our needs. On our property, we have natural springs, places where water from underground bedrocks called aquifers bubbles to the surface. This water overflows, nourishing the plants and small animals that draw from it. Along the edge of the springs, large trees shade the ground, which remains lush with ferns even when the rest of our yard is brown from drought. In the summer, the contrast is striking. The area closest to the springs remains vibrantly alive. The rest turns brown as it begins to die.

Figure 2.1

The Wellspring of Your Heart

Connected to the spring of living water

Bears fruit of love, grace, and truth

In Proverbs 4:23 Solomon used the imagery of the heart as a wellspring. Jeremiah referred to God as "the spring of living water" (2:13), the underground aquifer our hearts connect to. The aquifer is God's glory—an unfathomable, never-ending flow of love, grace, and truth. He sustains our spiritual being.

This wellspring imagery is a powerful metaphor. When we live with open hearts connected to this living water, God's love, grace, and truth provide life to our being. As we are nourished, we bear fruit providing opportunity for others to flourish. When we live from closed hearts, our connection to that living water is diminished. We begin to die and, in the absence of other channels of living water, those around us begin to die.

What does this mean practically? I mentioned earlier my prayer for an undivided heart. I would love to say that's no longer a struggle, but we all face daily choices that move us toward or away from deeper connection with God. I can generally tell when I'm battling a divided heart and leaning too heavily toward independence by the way I respond or am tempted to respond to others. When I'm short-tempered, judgmental, or unforgiving, it's an indication I haven't been connecting enough to God's heart, allowing his love to transform me. What comes out of me, then, isn't the life-giving water of God's love. It can actually lead to a degree of death within relationships and a lost opportunity to fulfill my purpose as an image bearer.

The more connected I am to God, the more I respond to others with kindness, compassion, and grace, inviting them to experience life through Christ in me. Whatever we fill our hearts with—whether things of God or of the world—is what flows out to others (see Luke 6:45).

This is why Solomon implores us to guard our hearts above all else.

What is it we guard our hearts against? Anything that separates us from God's love, because without the experience of his love, it is difficult to trust that God's heart toward us is good. In the absence of trust, we default to seeking our own desires.

In Eden, we first see the impact of failing to effectively guard the heart. In the battle of warring desires, did Adam and Eve choose,

Figure 2.2

The Wellspring of Your Heart

Disconnected from the spring of living water

Bears the fruit of sin and death

in humility, to trust God's desire for their lives? Or did they, even unintentionally, align with Evil's desire?

When Adam and Eve chose independence from God, their intimacy with God and each other shattered. God's image in them became distorted, the wellspring of their hearts marred by sin. Their capacity to fulfill their purpose—to reveal God's character—diminished. Their eyes opened, and for the first time they experienced shame—that inherent belief that something is wrong with us. Two human beings who had known only glory, tasted sin and fell short of the glory for which they were created (Romans 3:23).

Where once Adam and Eve walked and talked with God, they now hid. Where once they worked together in unity as rulers over creation, they now accused and blamed. What once was blessed came under curse. And as the fruit of sin grew, evil so permeated the human heart that in Noah's days the Lord noted that "every inclination of the thoughts of the human heart was only evil all the time," and the pain God experienced was so deep, he "regretted that he had made human beings" (Genesis 6:5–6).

Oh, how far human beings had fallen from the glory of Eden!

But God is gracious, and there is more to the story, his Larger Story of his love for creation.

Reconnection Through Christ

When our hearts disconnected from the Father at the fall, they became "deceitful… and beyond cure" (Jeremiah 17:9). But our compassionate Father would not abandon us to the fruit of our choices—a life consumed with fear and pride.

Knowing we could not bridge the divide our distrustful hearts created, God, in the most stunning, sacrificial expression of love ever demonstrated, crushed his own Son (Isaiah 53:10) to restore connection.

Jesus, fully human on this earth, was tempted as we are, but in the moment of greatest suffering, he trusted that his Father's heart toward him was good. Out of abundant love, he fulfilled his purpose through the sacrifice of his perfect life, which "made perfect those who are being made holy" (Hebrews 10:14 NLT).

When we respond to the pursuing love of God with repentance, turning from the Way of Pride to place our trust, love, and hope in the sacrificial gift of Christ, we are justified. The Father unites us to Christ, freeing us from the *penalty* of sin, and declares us righteous as he reconnects us to himself and adopts us into his family as beloved children.

Sanctification, or "being made holy," is the ongoing process of repentance and faith through which the Holy Spirit sets us free from the *power* of sin and restores us increasingly to the honor and glory

God created us for. We have the honor of revealing God's glory—his love, grace, and truth—through our attitudes and actions (Hebrews 2:9–11; Psalm 8:5–6).

Consummation comes as Christ returns for his beloved bride. Freed from the *presence* of sin, we will be honored to reign with him forever in a new heaven and earth even more glorious than Eden, fulfilling our part in God's Larger Story. This is why God created you!

The Lifelong Journey of Being Made Holy

Being made holy is a lifelong journey of being increasingly restored to the glory of who God created us to be as his image bearers. Though we've been redeemed—reconnected to the Father through Christ—our hearts still bear the effects of the fall. Fear and pride are often indicators of places where we are not rooted and grounded in God's love, resulting in a disconnect between what we rationally believe about God and what we are actually experiencing. This was the crux of my struggle in college when, in the face of fear and a lack of trust, I wrestled with choosing God's way over mine.

I didn't understand until years later that with my vulnerable prayer for an undivided heart, I essentially laid myself on the altar and invited a master surgeon to perform open heart surgery. Fear was a significant part of my story. It took decades of God gently exposing the ways I instinctively operated out of fear—seeking to meet my desires for safety, love, peace, and rest by controlling people and circumstances—before I could look back and see how God was answering that prayer. I wanted a quick fix: God, change my heart. He invited me instead into a deepening experience of his perfect love, which is the only antidote to fear.

As a teen, I loved God as completely as I knew how. But I see now that my knowing of his love was shallow based on what I perceived to be evidence of his love: answered prayers and having my needs and desires met. The problem with that immature understanding of love is that when God doesn't answer our prayers the way we want him to, we often default to thinking "God must not truly love or even like me" or whatever else it is we tell ourselves when we question God's love.

On my journey toward living from an undivided heart, I had to come to a place of trusting God's love for me regardless of my circumstances. That took time and repeatedly choosing to walk in the Way of Humility. It took opening my heart in trust in order to experience God's comfort in devastating disappointment, holding onto promises of his presence in seemingly hopeless places. In moving toward God in those spaces, I came to recognize that this is what love looks like: God being present with me in big ways and small ways, in my joys and my sorrows. In this, I came to a gut-level knowing that God can never act in a way that is unloving. And in that painful place where my definition of love and God's don't match, I can rest, trusting that, even still, I am loved no matter what happens.

This movement from fear and pride to trust and surrender is how we increasingly win the battle for our hearts. In fear, our hearts are disconnected—shut down and closed to the aquifer of God's love. But in trust, our hearts are connected and open to being loved. God's love nourishes us and empowers us to be who we're created to be, to love as we have been loved. This merging of divine intimacy, identity, and purpose creates opportunity not only for us to flourish, but for others to flourish as well. We saw it in Eden, we see it now, in part, and we will one day see it fully restored when God's glory fills the new earth and the new heavens.

What about you? Where do you see the battles in your own life? In what ways are you living out of fear and pride instead of fully trusting that God's heart toward you is good? Perhaps you find yourself trying to control or dominate others, consistently reacting out of anger or impatience, acting in ways contrary to your core values, overcommitting, overspending, pursuing your own desires at the expense of those around you. These are all indicators you are living out of fear rather than love.

If you do see some of these symptoms in your own thoughts and behavior, the path to change simply begins with awareness—with recognizing the times you act and react out of fear and pride. When this happens, you must choose, in humility, to open your vulnerable heart to the love of the Father and trust Him.

God reveals his love in multiple ways: through connection with his Spirit, connection with his Word, and connection with brothers and sisters who are willing to challenge us when we fall short of his glory and to call us to step into the fullness of who God created us to be. This is wholehearted community—believers in Christ coming together to experience and express God's love to him, one another, and the world. This type of community empowers us to win the battle for our hearts and step into our part in God's Larger Story.

Before we look more closely at this type of community, though, we need to consider the ways Evil hunts us to keep us disconnected from community with God and others and keep us from playing our part in God's Larger Story.

FOR DEEPER CONNECTION

Personalize

How does the imagery of your heart as a wellspring connect to your actual experience?

Gain Awareness

What happens in you as you think about the fact that becoming who you're created to be means simply living connected to God's love and letting it overflow to others?

Thinking of your heart as a wellspring that offers life to others, in what ways do you long to overflow more abundantly?

Respond

Heavenly Father, thank you for loving me so deeply that you sacrificed your Son so that I can live in relationship with you. In moments when I'm consumed by fear and doubt, help me to open my heart to experience the comfort of your love in its deepest parts. I want your love to reshape my understanding of who I am, so that I may live as the beloved image bearer you created me to be.

CHAPTER 3

Sculptures & Self-Protective Strategies

The always present battle for glory

Larry

In 2023, Mary and I celebrated my seventieth birthday and our fiftieth wedding anniversary during a trip to Italy. This gift from God fulfilled Mary's long-held dream of seeing the country's artistic and architectural wonders, particularly in Florence and Rome. We rejoiced in the extra gift of our son, Jonathan, joining us for part of the time.

A highlight of the trip was standing before Michelangelo's statue of David. I slowly walked around it to get a sense of its overwhelming presence. In awe, I beheld the brilliance and beauty of the sculpture—a robust young man, muscles bulging, and poised for attack—chiseled out of a flawed piece of marble. His sling and stone looked as if they were almost part of his body, his face confident and determined as he prepared to engage Goliath. You can see the fullness of David's magnificence because he is unclothed and without armor.

The story behind the statue starts with a young shepherd. David's father sends him to check on his older brothers in the army fighting the Philistines (see I Samuel 17). Arriving, David runs to the front lines to find the soldiers gripped with fear of the giant Goliath, unwilling to enter the battle. They saw a physical battle impossible to win. But David saw beyond the physical—he saw Goliath defying the armies of the living God. He saw that the real battle was about the glory of God being revealed through the people of God (v. 26).

So, how does this story relate to where you are in life? The most consequential battle you will ever fight—the battle for your heart—is being waged at all times, in all places, but the evidence of its existence is so subtle you could, like the Israelite army, be in the midst of it and fail to grasp its eternal significance. It's fought not with weapons honed of steel forged by human hands but by invisible forces in heavenly realms. And unlike most battles waged over temporal power, the stakes in the battle for your heart are infinitely higher.

Think about it for a moment. You may not be in physical battles, but when have you gotten frustrated with someone and lost sight of the fact that your words have impact beyond the moment? With your response you can reinforce the lies of Evil that keep someone steeped in pain and shame, or you can reveal God's grace and invite them to experience the healing and freedom found in his unconditional love.

The battles you face may look different than what David faced, but the stakes are the same: God's glory expressed through the wellspring of your heart. David clearly saw that this was what was at stake. So, what can we learn from his story about how to win the battles and overcome the giants in our own lives? The answer is in the statue.

The Way of Humility: The Power of a Vulnerable, Dependent Heart

Why Michelangelo chose to sculpt David naked for the world to see, other than it being typical of the Renaissance period, I can only speculate. Yet for me, I saw a critical element in David's victory: a heart of utter, vulnerable dependence.

As we saw in the last chapter, in the battle for God's glory, our hearts are the battlefield. So, Evil came after David's heart through the influential relationships of his oldest brother and Saul, the king of Israel. David's brother, filled with angry disdain, accused him of having a "conceited" and "wicked" heart (1 Samuel 17:28). The king looked at a young man inexperienced in battle and doubted David's capacity to fight a seasoned giant. Yet, David refused to believe the accusations of his brother or the doubts of his king.

What David believed deep within and confidently asserted is that the same God who empowered him to slay lions and bears to protect his father's sheep would empower him to slay a giant to protect the armies of Israel. This boldness flowed from an intimate knowing of who God was, who God created him to be, and what God created him to do, which was to reveal his glory.

After hearing David's confident declaration, the king blessed him and gave David his armor. David put it on, but it didn't fit him, so he rejected it.

The most critical element in David's eventual victory, Michelangelo could not fully capture: David's heart that believed God would deliver him. What Michelangelo could capture is David, naked and vulnerable, being who God created him to be, doing what God created him to do: a shepherd with a sling and five stones utterly trusting in God to reveal his glory. So, David courageously runs into the battle. With one well-placed stone David slays the giant, wins the battle, and reveals the glory of God!

Thousands of years later, that glory still shines vibrantly through the testimony of David's vulnerable dependency skillfully captured in white marble. As I beheld it, standing there with Jonathan and Mary, I saw what is truly at stake in the battle for my heart: simply being who God created me to be, doing what he created me to do, revealing his glory through naked, vulnerable dependence on him.

As I continued to reflect, the past flashed before me. I touched the pain of how, for much of my life, I didn't see the real battle and, as a result, I had often lived in pride and fear failing to reveal God's love, particularly to Jonathan and Mary. Then I felt an even deeper sense of gratitude for the last few decades of seeing the battle and increasingly opening my heart in vulnerable dependence upon God, empowering me to reveal his love to them on a deeper level.

How did I get to that place of deep gratitude?

The Way of Pride: The Costs of a Closed, Independent Heart

My life began when God knit me together in my mother's womb. Yet in the moment of conception, because of the fall, I experienced disconnection from God, my own heart, and the hearts of my parents. I tasted the fruit of Adam and Eve's fall from glory. As I got older, the Way of Pride—energized by fear—would, first subconsciously and eventually consciously, influence the way I answered my deepest heart questions:

> **Am I loved?**
> **Who am I?**
> **Why am I here?**

For most of my adult life I considered myself to have grown up in a loving, functional home. We were financially stable, and I had many opportunities in school and extracurricular activities to grow and develop. Yet, in my late forties, I realized my parents—from their own fallen families, in their fallen stories—could not give me all they longed to. Through my graduate program in Christian counseling, I began to see significant deficits in my experience of being emotionally connected, protected, and directed. In that lack, I saw how Evil whispered a subconscious message: *You are on your own to figure out your life, to answer the questions of your heart.*

In my natural temperament, intelligence, and internal drive, I became a high achiever. Achievement became my North Star, my internal compass for finding my way home to what I longed for but didn't really understand. Achievement slowly became my identity and purpose. It became my armor.

As Larry the Achiever, I subconsciously developed four strategies:

1. Stay in control
2. Help people
3. Get it right—whatever the "it" was I needed to accomplish
4. Do whatever it takes to come through to fulfill these strategies

These strategies were built upon natural, God-given talents. But in the battle for my heart, fear and pride distorted them. I subconsciously trusted them to be my armor—to protect me from the pain of rejection, failure, and harm—and fulfill my deepest desires for acceptance, emotional connection, safety, and significance.

This is a primary way Evil goes after us in the battle for our hearts: he tempts us to believe that in some way we can fulfill our deepest desires outside of utter dependence upon Christ. Take a moment to review below the key ways pride manifests itself in our lives.

Figure 3.0

The Way of Pride	
Independence	choosing what I want to do when I want to do it
Image management	projecting who I want to be/others want me to be
Indulgence	using my talents or self-medicating to meet my desires/avoid the pain of unmet desires
Self-inflation	elevating myself using my talents, possessions, or people
Energy: fear and control	
Result: disconnection, isolation	

Which of these elements of the Way of Pride do you see in your life? Perhaps several. Perhaps, like me, all of them!

The self-protective strategies we use in the Way of Pride often lead to success. In some cases, particularly in childhood, they may even be necessary for our survival. But eventually they sabotage our deepest desires because they are fear-driven, and fear keeps us disconnected from our hearts, God, and others.

In my teens and early adult years, my protective strategies worked well. In school I achieved academically and in extracurricular activities. I enjoyed public speaking, connecting, and being a leader in multiple settings. I felt known and respected by my peers and adults.

When I became a Christian, I quickly moved into leadership in church and in a regional youth ministry. I remember being a high school junior preaching the Sunday night service in a large church. Afterward, I asked the pastor for feedback. He was kind and gracious, but I now see that behind my questions was a desperate boy longing to know I came through.

Despite my biblically based knowledge that I was loved and accepted, deep within I consistently looked to people and experiences for a sense of significance. This was an early sign of the internal Larry the Achiever armor I had crafted without even knowing it: I was a teenager who achieved in order to get the affirmation and relational connection I longed for.

Mary and I were high school sweethearts and got married in college. After graduation, I went into financial consulting with a desire to honor God and love people well. But looking back, I can see that, again, without even realizing it, I was still Larry the Achiever, trying to stay in control, work hard, get it right, and do whatever it took to come through for my clients. That was a pretty good recipe for success. Most of the time people were pleased, my desires were met, and I avoided the pain of failure.

After thirteen years in business, God called us into pastoral ministry at a small, nondenominational church we had helped start years earlier. We focused on God's intimate love and care for us, our identity as beloved children in Christ, and our purpose to glorify

God by experiencing his love and expressing it to one another and the world.

We and our congregation experienced God's favor. We sought to live out our mission of being "a harbor of healing and sending." Yet, looking back, I can see that, once again, staying in control, working hard, getting it right, and doing whatever it takes to come through was a pretty good recipe for success. Despite the wonderful fruit of that season, all of my strategies, natural talent, and God's anointing could only temporarily cover up the distortions of fear and control.

As we clearly see in David's story, the soldiers drew back in fear; David moved forward in faith. Often, many of us—myself included—don't recognize the fear, so we don't even realize that part of our heart is shut down and that we are living independently of God. This limits our capacity to experience and express love to God and those we most long to connect with. Sometimes, our ignorance of fear and its effect can be devastating.

The Energy of Fear

As I look back, I can think of many examples of fear sabotaging my deepest desires and adversely affecting my relationships, the most painful memory being with our son, Jonathan.

As Jonathan grew up, we had many wonderful experiences. Mary was a devoted mother, and I worked hard to get it right as a father, to come through with my responsibilities, to give him what I didn't receive as a child, and, most of all, to protect him from the painful mistakes I had made growing up. I longed for him to have opportunities I didn't have, to experience the fullness of life God created him for.

During Jonathan's college years, a situation arose that brought Mary and me significant concern. As we prayed about it and consulted godly counsel, we decided to ask him to make a hard decision to change the situation. Of course we couched it in spiritual terms. He agreed to prayerfully consider our request and let us know his decision in several weeks when he returned from school.

I'll never forget the internal tension and anxiety of wondering what he had decided. When he arrived and we had time to discuss it, Jonathan was surprised by my concern. His response was, "How could I disagree with you and the other godly men you consulted?" I was relieved and grateful.

Our relationship with Jonathan seemed to go back to where it had been. But gradually Mary and I saw changes we didn't understand. Little did we know that in my pressure and his compliance, seeds were growing that would eventually bring forth devastating consequences.

Several years after he graduated, Jonathan and I met in a coffee shop in the city where he worked. I don't even remember how it came up, but I clearly remember him referring to that decision he had made at my prompting. He had come to believe that I had acted out of fear and control, and that belief negatively impacted him and our relationship. I immediately responded that I didn't think I had, but I'd consider whether that might be true.

The next day, I was contemplating our conversation when it hit me. Yes! I had acted out of fear, fear that he would repeat my mistakes and experience the pain I longed for him to avoid. However, even after seeing this reality, it would take me a long time to fully recognize and own the magnitude of the impact.

My parenting out of fear and control contributed to Jonathan, in his thirties, rebelling against a lifetime of complying to others' expectations, making a series of choices that ultimately led to a divorce. This brought devastating consequences to him, his wife Laurie, his five children, and to us as parents and grandparents. The pain I feared had exponentially come upon us all.

Through all of this I began to more fully face the pain and cost of parenting from unrecognized fear and pride. Fear drove me to exercise inappropriate control. Fear blocked authentic connection. Fear distorted and sabotaged my deepest desires to love and protect. I was not responsible for Jonathan's choices, but I was responsible for the seedbed from which the disconnect in my own heart grew.

The Disconnect

For years I was a man seeking to love God and love others. I knew the biblical truth of God's love for me and my identity and purpose in Christ. But I couldn't see the disconnected places in my heart that were indicators I was losing the battle for my heart. This disconnect was the difference between the biblical truth I rationally agreed with and tried hard to act out of and the false visceral beliefs that I often reacted out of in the moment of pressure. These beliefs sabotaged what I most longed for.

A false belief is anything that is not consistent with the biblical revelation of God's love, grace, and truth about God, us, others, and life itself. It is any argument or "lofty opinion raised against the knowledge of God" (see 2 Corinthians 10:5 ESV). A false visceral belief is one that is formed in the hidden depths of our hearts, often at a subconscious level. In the shutdown, independent parts of my heart these beliefs ultimately formed Larry the Achiever.

So, in my moment of pressure with Jonathan, without recognizing it, I chose what I viscerally believed—*it's up to me to keep my son from making a mistake and save him from pain*. Then, I acted out of fear that led to control.

What was the impact? I sabotaged what I most longed to be: a man who reveals God's love, who protects and provides, particularly for Mary and Jonathan. That is heartbreaking. Through the process of becoming wholehearted—connecting to my heart, God's heart, and the hearts of others—I slowly came to understand the disconnect and see the false visceral beliefs that built the armor of Larry the Achiever. I saw how Evil deceived me—just as he deceived Adam and Eve—into believing that my deepest desires could be met in myself, others, or experiences instead of in utter dependence upon God. Then I acted out of independence, fear, and control. Here is a simple diagram of how this worked out in my life.

Figure 3.1

Larry the Achiever

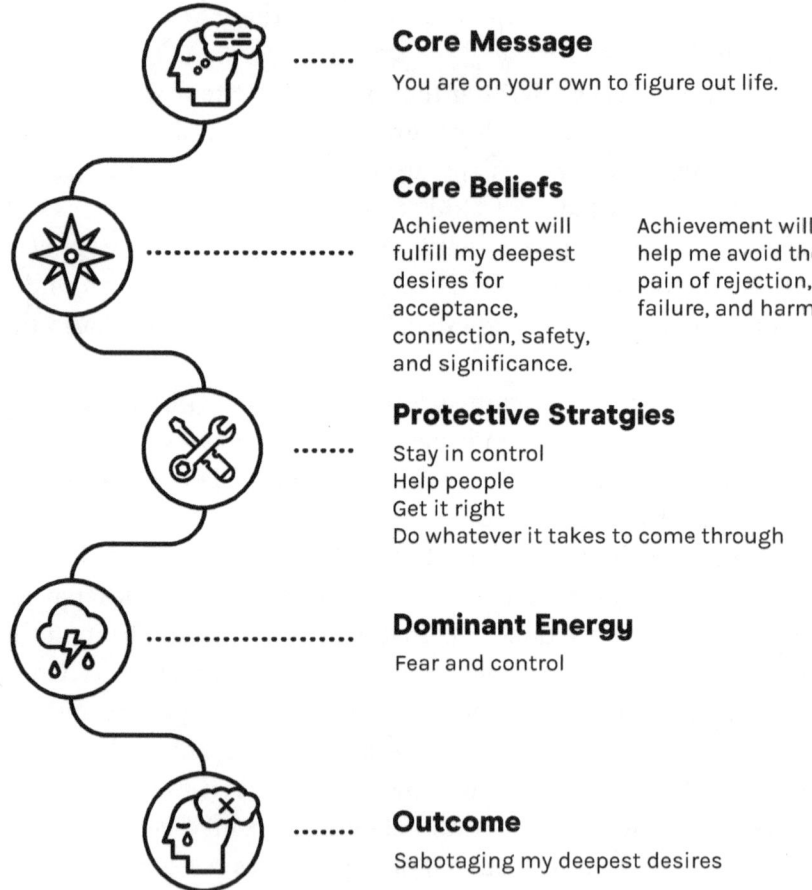

Core Message
You are on your own to figure out life.

Core Beliefs
Achievement will fulfill my deepest desires for acceptance, connection, safety, and significance.

Achievement will help me avoid the pain of rejection, failure, and harm.

Protective Stratgies
Stay in control
Help people
Get it right
Do whatever it takes to come through

Dominant Energy
Fear and control

Outcome
Sabotaging my deepest desires

As you read my story and review this diagram, I wonder what might connect to your story. In the last few weeks, how might you identify with being in moments of pressure and acting out of fear and control instead of the biblical truth you know and long to act out of?

Closing the Disconnect

So how can I, a man who loves God with a wonderful biblical knowledge about God, myself, and others be set free from the deception of Larry the Achiever? How can I fulfill my deep desire to live from biblical truth, honor God, and be the man he created me to be?

To close the disconnect we must discover our whole hearts for it is in the depths of our hearts, as we said in chapter 2, that we determine to whom or what we give our trust, hope, and love. In that ongoing process, I discovered the painful reality that the prophet Jeremiah knew,

> The heart is deceitful above all things and beyond cure. Who can understand it?
> "I the LORD search the heart and examine the mind, to reward each person according to their conduct, according to what their deeds deserve." (Jeremiah 17:9–10)

The terms *heart* and *mind* Jeremiah refers to in these verses covers "the range of hidden elements in man's character and personality."[4]

To deeply trust God, hope in him, and love him in a way that changes the way we act, we must discover and go into the hidden depths of our hearts. As theologian Dr. Robert Saucy, said:

> One of the greatest hindrances to our healing and growth is leaving the issues that trouble our life and stifle our transformation hidden and unknown in the depth of our heart, split off from our conscious thought. **So long as we think that we believe something, but the real thought in the depth of our heart is different, we will never experience personal transformation** (emphasis mine).[5]

How do we go into these hidden depths of our hearts? We humbly cry out like David for God to search our hearts (see Psalm 139:23–24). He searches our hearts through the scriptures that are "sharper than any two-edged sword… discerning the thoughts and intentions of the heart" (Hebrews 4:12 ESV). As we open our hearts to God's Word, he "probes the inmost recesses of our spiritual being and brings the subconscious motives to light."[6]

Sometimes the discovery of the hidden places of our hearts comes through others who have the courage to speak the truth in love. People we trust who draw upon God's Word to help us recognize when the truth we say we believe doesn't line up with our actions—actions that flow from our false visceral beliefs. When Jonathan challenged my actions and shared the impact of them, the Spirit brought to light "subconscious motives" that sabotaged what I most longed for.

As we discover the hidden depths of our hearts we begin to face where we, in pride and fear, place our trust in ourselves, people, or experiences. Like Paul, we find ourselves failing to do the good we desire and actually doing what we don't want to do (see Romans 7:15).

When we begin to face what we believe deep within and the costs of those beliefs, it is painful, and it needs to be! But then the Spirit guides us—in utter desperation—to see with Paul the grace of God: "Thank God! The answer is in Jesus Christ our Lord" (v. 25 NLT). A drastic problem requires a drastic solution, so God sent his Son to share in our humanity that he might cure our deceitful hearts through his sacrificial life, death, and resurrection (see Hebrews 2:14–18; Jeremiah 17: 9–10).

Two Paths: Which Will You Choose?

In the Way of Pride, we choose independence—like Larry the Achiever. Out of fear of pain or the desire for pleasure, we choose the armor of self-protection. In the Way of Pride, we put our love and trust in ourselves, others, and a multitude of experiences that we hope will satisfy our deepest desires and answer our deepest questions but never will.

In the Way of Humility, we choose vulnerable dependence on God in whom we put our love, trust, and hope—like David and Paul. As we increasingly discover and open the hidden places of our hearts to the lordship of Christ, we become rooted and grounded in love. The disconnect begins to close as the biblical truth we rationally agree with and long to obey increasingly becomes visceral reality. We experience our deepest desires being satisfied as we experience and express the love of God overflowing to his glory.

Which path you take determines the extent to which you will win the battle for your heart to become the person God created you to be. In a battle over God's glory where the battlefield is your heart, will you cooperate with Evil—either consciously or subconsciously—to diminish and distort the glory of God flowing through you? Or will you choose to surrender to God and become a free-flowing channel of his glory?

Figure 3.2

The Wellspring of Your Heart

Which will you choose?

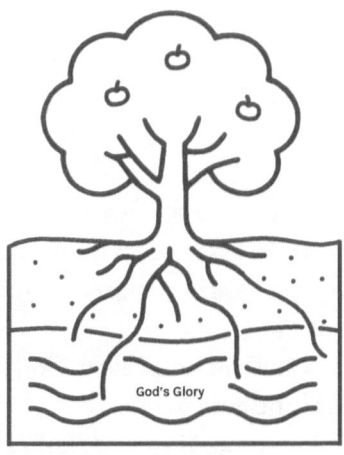

The Way of Humility

The Way of Pride

As a young shepherd David chose the Way of Humility, revealing the glory of God by slaying Goliath and rescuing the people of God. But in his later years, King David chose the Way of Pride. Despite his abundance, somehow, he believed God's love and blessings were not enough. He wanted more. He despised the Word of the Lord by taking what he wanted, when he wanted it. He killed Uriah and took his wife, Bathsheba, for himself (see 2 Samuel 11–12).

As God dramatically confronted David through the prophet Nathan, David embraced humility by confessing his sin and vulnerably opening the depths of his heart to let God's love and truth fill his inward being, teaching him "wisdom in the secret heart" (Psalm 51:6 ESV). David was then able to experience "the joy of [his] salvation" showing other sinners like us the way back home (vv. 12–13).

When we, like David, respond to the Father's loving correction with humility, we can experience God redeeming parts of our broken stories. During and after Jonathan's divorce, we all faced in different ways the painful consequences of our own choices. As we grieved and repented of our part, God gave Mary and me the opportunity to parent in a profoundly different way than we had in his childhood and through college.

Through radical, vulnerable dependence upon the community of the Spirit, the Word, and brothers and sisters who walked with us, we discovered how to imperfectly but consistently reveal the Father's unconditional love, grace, and truth to our prodigal son. As Jonathan experienced us loving differently, he slowly began to come home to his own heart and our hearts. He began to open to the love of faithful friends. In this community of love, Jonathan came home to his heavenly Father who led him to radically pursue the hearts of his family. As he did, God opened Laurie's heart to respond in humility. Four years after their divorce, Jonathan and Laurie remarried and united their family in a whole new way of life.

That day as I stood in Florence with Jonathan and Mary, God's gracious kindness flashed before me. His kindness to close the disconnect in the heart of a profoundly broken man, husband, father, and grandfather; his kindness to empower each of us to let go of our armor and move into the battle in radical, vulnerable, naked dependence upon God's grace; his kindness to open Laurie's heart to a miracle of grace.

I stood there overwhelmed with gratitude to our kind Father who is taking the flawed marble of our lives and sculpting something glorious!

The Way of Humility is painful, long, and often hard. It begins when you surrender to divine love, open your heart, and let the love of Christ fill even the hidden places. Then you can walk through the darkest times of suffering, trusting God to bring forth glory in this life or the next. This is the path to becoming wholehearted, to experiencing the fullness of life we long for. It begins with discovering your whole heart.

FOR DEEPER CONNECTION

Personalize

When have you responded out of self-protection in ways that created a sense of distance from God or others? (See Way of Pride chart for common self-protective strategies.)

Gain Awareness

When you've operated out of fear and pride, how has it impacted you becoming who you're created to be?

What would freedom or growth look like in this area?

Respond

Heavenly Father, help me recognize more quickly those times when I create space between you and myself by choosing pride and independence. I come to you humble and dependent, choosing to believe the truth that you love me, you see me, and you long for a relationship with me.

Part 2

Overcoming Obstacles to Connection

Moving from disconnection to connection with your own heart, God, and others

CHAPTER 4

Colorful Socks

What choices reveal about the true state of your heart

Anisa

Discovering your whole heart is a deeply personal journey not only into the hidden places of your own heart, but into the heart of a God who longs to reveal himself when we seek him with our whole heart (Jeremiah 29:13). I could not have known, when I embarked on the path to becoming wholehearted, how much more I would come to know of God's kindness, his compassion, his sacrificial love, and his unmerited grace in the face of my brokenness.

Nor did I recognize, at the start, the true extent of loss I experienced through years of living unaware of my heart.

I remember as a teenager watching *St. Elmo's Fire* when Demi Moore, slumped against a wall looking forlorn, uttered a statement which lingered in my memory long after: "I never thought I'd be so tired at twenty-two."

What captured my attention was that it wasn't physical weariness she referred to. She emanated a kind of world weariness and disillusionment I wouldn't have imagined I'd encounter in someone so young. She was just a handful of years older than I was at the time and already the dreams around the future she'd envisioned were beginning to tarnish.

In hindsight I see how closely this movie character's experience foreshadowed my own reality. Maybe not to the exact year, but certainly not far removed. It seemed much of my mid-twenties to early thirties were more about surviving than thriving.

By my early thirties, the demands of being a wife, a homeschool mom, and part-time employee coupled with church and extended family obligations weighed heavily. My go-to manner of coping was to shove down anything resembling attention to my own feelings and desires and instead focus on the next thing that needed to be done, the next person who needed to be cared for. I'd come to the unavoidable conclusion that life is hard—much harder than it looks through the lens of adolescence—and all the "hard" of life fell squarely on my adult shoulders. I remember a passing conversation with my husband once as I half-jogged through a department store to avoid connecting with anything appealing vying for my attention.

"I never go to stores like these," I threw out.

"Why?" he asked.

"Because then I won't see things I might want."

Our budget didn't allow for wants, so my protective strategy was not to allow myself to *want* anything.

I didn't understand the ramifications of gradually cutting myself off from my desires until a few years later when I was filling out an online survey about what kind of socks I liked.

Did I like colorful socks? *Yes.*

Did I like socks with designs? *Yes.*

Did I like this kind of sock? Did I like that kind of sock? *Yes, yes, and yes again.*

As I answered question after question, I felt the excitement building in me about all the wonderful socks out there. And then I got to the last question: "What kind of socks do you have in your drawer?"

Plain, white socks.

For some reason, this hit me with the force of running into a brick wall. Even more than a decade later, I remember the feeling and the accompanying thought, *How can I be so out of touch with what I like that I won't even spend five dollars on a pair of colorful socks?*

Moving from Disconnection to Connection with Your Heart

What difference does it make if we're out of touch with our hearts? Out of touch, as I was, with our desires? For people who are created in the image of a relational God, created for connection with God and others, it makes a significant difference. As John Calvin offers in *Institutes of the Christian Religion*:

> Nearly all the wisdom which we possess, that is to say, true and sound wisdom, consists of two parts: the knowledge of God and of ourselves. But, while joined by many bonds, which one precedes and brings forth the other is not easy to discern.[7]

According to Calvin, knowledge of God and knowledge of oneself are inextricably linked. To know God, we must know ourselves and to know ourselves, we must know God.

Relationships are interdependent by nature. Knowing and connecting with our hearts is critical to knowing and connecting to the hearts of God and others. Wholehearted living is like a delicate dance: we respond to God's pursuing love by opening our hearts to experience love. As we experience love, we gain courage to open our hearts further, allowing deeper connection with God and others. In this process, we increase our capacity not only to experience love but also express it through the wellspring of our hearts.

This is an often-missed piece in the Great Commandment in Luke 10:27: "'Love the Lord your God with all your heart and with all your soul and with all your strength and with all your mind'; and 'Love your neighbor as *yourself*'" (emphasis mine). While we focus on loving God and others, we often overlook the importance of being loved ourselves.

But it is in *being* loved that we gain capacity *to* love. If we don't open our whole hearts to receive love, we cannot effectively love because we cannot give what we have not experienced. As John says, "We love because he first loved us" (1 John 4:19).

So, how do we live from an integrated or whole heart? The first step begins with understanding the four levels of our hearts—our desires, feelings, thoughts, and choices—and identifying areas of internal disconnection.

During most of the first three decades of my life, for instance, my walk with the Lord was about serving God and serving others. I paid little attention to what was going on inside my heart.

When I attended my first Battle for the Heart weekend at Wellspring Group and was introduced to the life-changing concept of living from a whole heart, I understood for the first time that my heart was important and that by ignoring parts of my heart, I wasn't loving myself. I understand now that loving others as you love yourself requires you to *love yourself* (see Luke 10:27; Matthew 22:37–39; Mark 12:30–31), and that involves *caring* for your whole heart, including being attentive to your feelings and desires—the parts of myself I'd long ignored.

When I realized that desires were a good thing, that they were given to me by God, it became one of the most transformational experiences of my life. As I got in touch with my desires, it felt like slowly coming alive again after years of ignoring and denying vital parts of myself. As I accepted that my desires were part of me and shouldn't be rejected, as I paid attention to them, it fed something vital within me: a desire to do more than just survive, but to thrive! I realized much of my prior motivation for doing the "right" things came from well-intentioned desires to please and help others, but those desires became distorted when I chose to do so at the expense of myself. And that left me with little energy to do the things I was most passionate about, those things I felt created for. But living from a place of deep desire—in alignment with God's desires—energized me. My deep desires became something like directional signs I used when seeking God's plan for my life. They empowered me to say no to being all things to all people so I could embrace being the woman God created me to be.

Moving from a heart that is partly shut down—where you give little to no attention to one or more of the four parts—to a heart that is integrated is not an overnight event. Just as I spent years gradually shutting down my heart, I have spent years reintegrating. Part of that has been learning to sit in my feelings and desires, to allow myself to experience them rather than note them in passing. It's the difference in knowing what a car is because you've seen one in a picture versus sitting inside one, feeling the stiff-backed seats, smelling the leather, and hearing the engine purr.

The process of reintegrating our hearts is much like strengthening little-used muscles. Initially it takes intentional focus to even become aware of what you are experiencing, but eventually the recognition becomes fluid, and you can process through all four parts quickly, much like an elevator that moves smoothly from one floor to the next.

We use an elevator to illustrate the four levels, or functions, of the heart because it presents each part, or floor, as distinct but illustrates that there is movement between the parts. In contrast to the elevator's linear movement, though, the four levels of the heart are interconnected, and our movement between the levels is more circular than linear. The elevator model of the heart provides a helpful visual demonstrating conscious integration of the heart.

Figure 4.0

**Elevator Model
of the Heart**

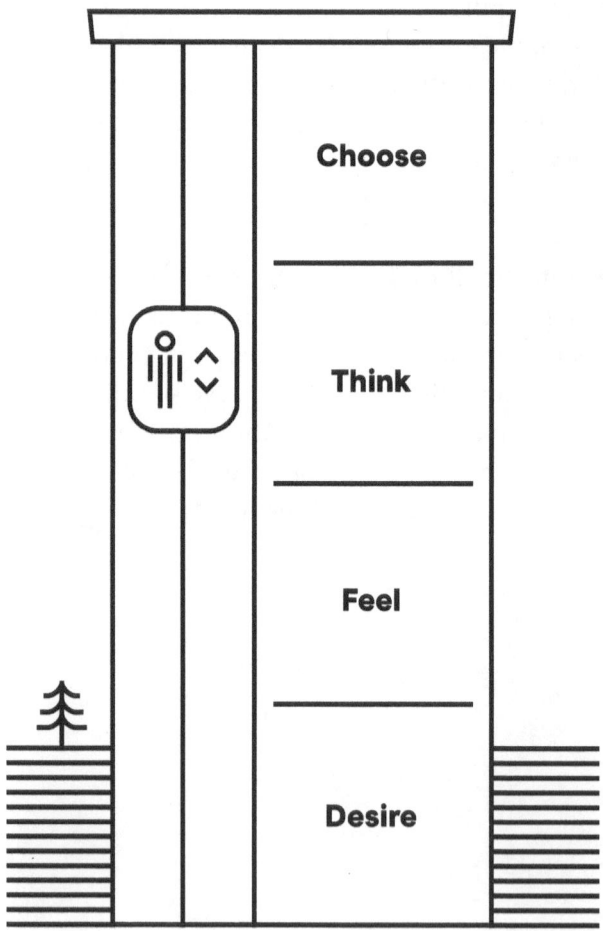

The Four Levels of the Heart

All of us have some degree of heart integration. We act and react out of deep desires as well as experience feelings, even if we don't acknowledge them. But when we move toward conscious integration, we recognize our desires, feelings, and thoughts, and then choose out of the deep desires God has placed in us. Integration leads to agency. We have choices and we can either choose to respond out of our whole hearts or react out of hearts that are partially disconnected.

Floor 1: Desires

At the core of our beings, we are people who desire, and those desires drive everything we do.

When we mention desires and that they are God-given, a lot of people have an initial negative reaction. In our society, desires have come to be associated primarily with sexual desire or selfishness. Additionally, for Christians, there is confusion around verses related to evil desires and pain. We read "You were taught, with regard to your former way of life, to put off your old self, which is being corrupted by its deceitful desires" (Ephesians 4:22), and we wonder, "Does that mean all desires are evil?" We struggle to reconcile verses such as "Delight yourself in the LORD, and he will give you the desires of your heart" (Psalm 37:4 ESV).

Many misunderstandings about desires arise because we don't realize there are different types of desires. In the case of warring desires, the answer is not to kill desire, but to allow God to purify our desires so our deepest desires reflect his desires.

There are three main types of desires:

Surface desires are those we can most easily identify and are what we most commonly think about when we talk about desires. Surface desires can be material (such as the desire for colorful socks), positional (I want a promotion at work), relational (to have a friend or be married), or experiential (I long to take a vacation). Surface desires are not inherently selfish or wrong, though some can be. They are helpful tools in connecting us to our deeper desires.

Deceptive desires are surface desires we mistakenly believe will satisfy a deep desire or answer our deepest questions. For example, it's when we think a promotion will give us a sense of purpose and fully satisfy our deep desire to feel valued, seen, or to have impact or that a specific relationship will fully satisfy our desire to feel loved. Having a surface desire met can provide satisfaction, but it is temporary and often leads to a compulsive need to have more to feed the unmet deeper desire. We saw this brought out in the story of Larry the Achiever.

Deep desires are the deepest longings of the human heart. They are given to us by God to draw us to himself. Our deep desires can only be fully satisfied through wholehearted connection to God, ultimately in eternity. Until then, we get increasing glimpses and tastes of that fulfillment in our connection with God, others, and life itself.

Deep desires include:

- **Purpose**—to be part of something larger; to have transcendence or glory
- **Relationship**—to experience connection through community or family; to love and be loved, to pursue and be pursued
- **Impact**—to have significance
- **Honor**—to be respected
- **Value**—to be seen, known, and understood
- **Security**—to be safe; to protect and provide or to be protected and provided for
- **Duty**—to come through, to hear "Well done!"
- **Beauty and Creativity**—to experience and create beauty

- **Truth and Justice**—to see all human beings valued and respected; to see right and good prevail
- **Freedom**—to have the right and capacity to freely choose
- **Adventure**—to engage in an exciting, often risky endeavor for a captivating vision or reward
- **Peace and Rest**—to experience wholeness, completion, home, order
- **Joy**—to experience pleasure and satisfaction from desires met
- **Personal Agency**—to exercise appropriate self-control

In my story, my surface desire for colorful socks was tied to deeper desires for beauty and value. Over the course of several years, I have come to see that the desire for beauty, which I once thought wasn't significant to me, is one of the deepest desires of my heart. I experience beauty in nature, writing, and simple things such as colorful socks.

Deep desires transcend gender, race, and socioeconomic standing. It is this type of desire the psalmist mentioned when he wrote that God will give you the desires of your heart. It isn't about material things. It's not that God doesn't care about meeting those desires; he longs to bless us. But when God meets our surface desires, those blessings are meant to be a signpost pointing us to him and the ultimate satisfaction which can only be found in him. For example, as I have come to understand my desire for beauty, I have increasingly connected to God through the beauty of nature. One day, walking at sunset, looking at the changing colors, it hit me what a gift it is that God placed us in a world where we can always connect to the beauty of creation, if only by looking up. In that moment, I felt connected to God and overwhelmed with his love, seeing the extravagant lengths he would go to in reminding me he cares for me.

Floor 2: Feelings

The words *feelings* and *emotions* are often used interchangeably, but there is a subtle difference. Emotions are our body's instinctive reaction to what we experience and are largely subconscious.

Feelings, on the other hand, are how we make sense of our emotional responses. For example, if you see a snake, you might have an immediate emotional response of fear that you're in danger, accompanied by a racing heart. But when you stop to interpret what you're seeing and experiencing, you might feel relief when you realize the snake is harmless and you are safe.

Feelings flow out of our perceptions of how our desires are either being met or blocked. For example, in the snake illustration, the desire was for safety. When desires are met, we experience feelings such as relief, pleasure, joy, or satisfaction. When desires are blocked, we experience feelings such as fear, frustration, and anger.

It may help to think of feelings as indicator lights on the dashboard of your heart. When I see the check engine light come on in my car, I know something is going on under the hood. If I ignore it too long, the engine could quit or even blow up, leaving significant collateral damage.

In the same way, our feelings are God's dashboard lights revealing what is going on in the engine of our hearts.

Floor 3: Thoughts

All of us are familiar with this floor! The thoughts level is generally considered to be the realm of conscious knowing where we observe, analyze, and draw conclusions about ourselves, others, and all of life. But as we discussed in chapter 3, we're not always aware of the subconscious thoughts that impact our choices.

Although our thoughts are represented as a single level on the elevator, we access this level at each stage of processing as we identify our desires, feelings, and choices and try to make sense of them. For example, in this moment, if I stop to get in touch with what I'm feeling, I can identify that I'm feeling impatient. When I try to make sense of why I'm feeling impatient, I access the thoughts level. I am impatient because I desire to walk outside to enjoy the nice spring weather, but I also desire to finish editing this chapter. Then, as I continue thinking, I realize that underneath both desires is the deep desire for rest. Ultimately, I decide the best way to experience rest is to finish the task and then go outside.

Floor 4: Choices

The choices level is at the top of the elevator because it is the outworking of what we desire, feel, and think. We choose based on how we consciously or subconsciously process our desires, feelings, and thoughts.

Many of us take a think-choose approach to change. I should change, so I choose to _____ (whatever your action step is). This is the least effective approach to lasting change. Instead, getting in touch with our deep desires gives us energy for change. For example, on any given day when I consider exercising, it generally starts with the thought "I should exercise." The "why" behind my thought is that I know it's good for me. But that's not enough to motivate me to choose to exercise. So, if I stop at the thoughts and choices level, I'm just as likely not to exercise as I am to exercise. However, when I get in touch with my deep desires, there are two that increase the likelihood I'll follow through to virtually 100 percent. Relational connection—getting to exercise with someone else—or my desire to have a full, healthy life even as I age.

God gives every human being a will and a desire for agency—the ability to make free choices. But our capacity to exercise that ability varies based on temperament and the internal beliefs we've developed through life experiences. The more we discover and know our hearts, the freer we are to effectively choose what we most deeply desire.

Understanding the Levels of Your Heart

Now that we've looked at the four levels of the heart, pause and consider:

- What level of the elevator do you most often operate from?
- What level do you access the least?
- What do you think might be different in your life if you lived, consistently, from all four levels?

We cannot win the battle for our hearts if we don't understand our hearts. Becoming wholehearted is about living increasingly connected to all four parts of our hearts so we can more fully experience and express God's love as we live in deep, authentic life-giving relationship with him and others. This is a depth of relational connection many of us have never known.

How do we get there? The process of integrating the four levels of your heart takes time and practice. But it's something you can begin today by using our State of Your Heart reflection tool.

This tool—along with a Desires Chart and a Feelings Chart—is included in the Toolbox at the end of the book and downloadable on our website at becomingwholehearted.org. Sample State of Your Heart updates are also on the website.

To use this tool:

- Pick a situation with emotional content, positive (such as a friend celebrating your birthday) or negative (such as being passed over for a promotion).
- Answer the questions provided, taking time to carefully consider what is going on inside you.
- Don't worry about getting it right—there are no wrong answers. All feelings, even those we categorize as negative, are valid. Each connects back to a met or unmet deep desire.

I'm going to illustrate this tool using a situation I processed several years ago. This situation shows the change I've experienced moving from someone who consciously chose to shut down part of my heart to avoid pain to someone who now seeks to take my pain and the underlying deep desires to God with an open heart.

Describe the situation

I was scheduled to leave this morning for a retreat where I'll be facilitating a small group. My husband got up for work while I stayed in bed half asleep. When he was ready to leave, he gave me a quick kiss and left without saying anything. I immediately woke up and felt hurt when I realized he left without praying for me, something he normally does when I travel.

What am I thinking?

Why didn't he pray for me? I know it shouldn't be a big deal. He wasn't trying to hurt my feelings. He probably forgot. But it's significant to me when he prays for me. I feel cared for, not alone. He's part of the spiritual covering God has placed in my life, so in some ways, I feel unprotected.

What am I feeling?

Sad. Missed. Unsafe, unprotected. Angry (flowing out of the pain). Uncertain regarding how I should respond.

What am I desiring?

Surface desire—to be prayed for
Deceptive desire—to stay angry so he sees how he hurt me
Deep desires—to be seen, cared for, loved. To be protected.

What do I want to choose?

Honestly, I just want to stay angry or ignore him like I feel ignored. But I also don't want to be that kind of person. I know that I can't turn to my husband to meet all my needs. So, I need to find a way to take those unmet desires to God and ask him to meet them. I'm choosing to spend some time in prayer processing what I'm feeling and expressing my disappointment and asking God to comfort me, to be my protector and the one who sees and cares for me even when I feel missed by my husband.

After going through this process, I chose to pray, asking God to be my secure place and pouring out my pain and longing. As I did, I experienced his comfort washing over me as he reminded me of the truth that I am not alone. He will never leave me or forsake me. I felt seen, loved, and protected. That enabled me to get up and go about my routine with a sense of connection to God, and surprisingly, to my husband as my anger dissipated. I could accept his love as it was offered without resenting him for not being something he was never intended to be—my primary source of security.

Later that morning my husband did call and pray for me. He mentioned that he had not done so earlier because he didn't want to wake me. In this, I felt seen by him and God—something I wouldn't have experienced if my heart was shut down.

Walking through the State of Your Heart exercise helped me integrate my heart and make choices out of my deep desire to be who God created me to be, someone who responds out of love rather than pride, fear, or anger.

Reflecting on the state of your heart is a spiritual discipline in which we invite God to search our hearts and reveal the hidden depths (Psalm 139:23; Proverbs 20:27). To open your heart, even to yourself, feels vulnerable. It requires choosing the Way of Humility as you face your own pain and brokenness.

Using the State of Your Heart tool will help you

- recognize and engage in the battle for your heart as you consider how your choices lead to internal connection (integration) or disconnection;
- identify specific ways Evil hunts you to keep you disconnected through fear and pride;
- increasingly win the battle for your heart as you exercise agency, making conscious choices based on the person you want to be;
- gain capacity to connect with God at a whole heart level that you might more fully experience his love, grace, and truth;
- fight for the hearts of others as you increasingly become an expression of God's love, grace, and truth to the world;
- become who God created you to be.

As Larry and I have said before, change like this doesn't happen overnight. So be patient. God is at work restoring the wellspring of your heart. And he is committed to doing whatever it takes for you to more fully experience his love, even—as Larry shares in the next chapter—if restoration comes in the form of blowing up internal dams that have been blocking the flow of his love from entering into and through the wellspring of your heart.

FOR DEEPER CONNECTION

Personalize

As you consider living from a whole heart—attentive to your desires, feelings, thoughts, and choices—what are you discovering about yourself?

Gain Awareness

What would it be like if you could more consistently live from a whole heart—even in places of pain—trusting that God will meet you there? Try to include at least one feeling word in your answer. (See Feelings chart in the Toolbox.)

What deep desire(s) would it touch if you lived this way? (See Desires chart in the Toolbox.)

Respond

Father, you created me to live, love, and be loved at a whole heart level. I confess, though, that living so vulnerably can feel scary. Help me entrust my heart to you and open it fully to your love so that I can open it to others.

CHAPTER 5

Demolishing Dams

Beliefs that block connection

Larry

In May 2000, I was in my eleventh year as pastor of a small-town church. One evening while participating with another church in special meetings, a dear friend came up to me. During the service, she'd sensed the Lord had given her an insight about me—a mental image she wanted to share.

"Larry," she told me, "I saw something like the Hoover Dam inside of you. Just like the Hoover Dam stops up a river, there is something inside you that is holding back the flow of God's Spirit through you."

I clearly remember where we stood and how her words seemed to communicate something was wrong with me. My internal response? "Who do you think you are?"

But I knew this woman, I respected her, so I put on my nice pastoral persona and said, "I really appreciate that. I'll pray about it."

That was a dangerous commitment. After thirty-two years walking with God, I longed to truly know him and for his Spirit to flow freely through my heart. So, despite my internal resistance, I took a deep breath and asked God to reveal any hidden dams in my life. Little did I know what was coming in the next nineteen months! God would answer that prayer through a painful process of exposing the hidden places of my heart where the Way of Pride acted like a dam diminishing the flow of God's Spirit to and through me. How did this dam form?

Forming dams

In reality, *all* of us have internal dams, those areas of disconnection in our relationship with God that block the flow of his love to and through us. Places where our rational, biblically based understanding of God's love isn't able to penetrate the depths of our hearts and being. They often come in the form of false visceral beliefs, touched on in chapter 3, that are radically opposed to what we know to be biblically true. They become apparent in areas where we find ourselves struggling to overcome sinful and destructive patterns of behavior.

How do these disconnections form?

Our gut-level beliefs are formed at the intersection of our desires, feelings, thoughts, and choices, often outside of conscious awareness and often in childhood. They are formed through our experiences and the ways we consciously or subconsciously interpret them.

Figure 5.0

How Visceral Beliefs Are Formed

The gut-level beliefs we act from under pressure

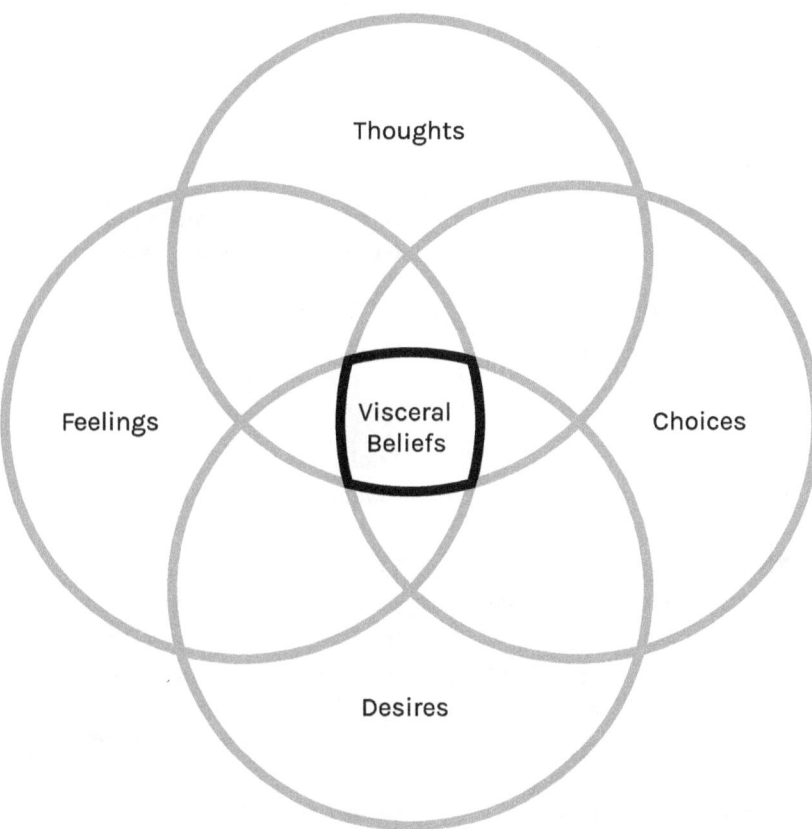

Sometimes a belief forms from a single, traumatic event. Other times it may be a series of seemingly minor experiences, even positive ones, that communicate a message over time.

To see how a belief forms, we'll use an illustration separating each heart level to understand its importance and how the levels work together. In this example, when we speak of desires, we aren't referring to needs that sustain physical life. Yet many of these desires are actual needs in infants and have powerful impact into adulthood because they play a part in answering our essential heart questions.

Figure 5.1

A child whose basic needs are met	A child whose basic needs are NOT met
Desires to be cared for, nurtured, safe	**Desires** to be cared for, nurtured, safe
Feels seen, safe, secure, loved	**Feels** unseen, unsafe, insecure, unloved
Thinks consciously or subconsciously. Processes the experience and concludes: if I cry out, my needs will be met. Someone will be there for me.	**Thinks** consciously or subconsciously. Processes the experience and concludes: if I cry out, my needs will not be met. No one will be there for me. I must meet my own needs.
Chooses to trust their caregiver to meet their needs.	**Chooses** to distrust their caregiver and do whatever is necessary to meet their own needs.

In this illustration, the first child's heart is open to trust their caregiver, but a part of the second child's heart subconsciously shuts down in distrust of their caregiver. How might their experiences impact them when they are older and choose to surrender their lives to Christ?

When they become a Christian, they may adopt a biblical worldview that they accept as truth, but that doesn't automatically override their lived experience. A person who's spent a lifetime struggling to trust others will continue that struggle even in their relationship with God. For change to occur, God's love, grace, and truth have to permeate our whole hearts where beliefs are formed.

In this simple illustration, positive life experiences developed trust and negative life experiences led to distrust. However, we all struggle with trust to a degree because we all bear the trauma of separation due to the fall. Additionally, even positive life experiences can lead to the formation of false visceral beliefs. A child could receive significant affirmation while growing up, being praised for their kindness, intelligence, and personal achievement. These positive reinforcements, which are appropriate and well intended, can communicate subtle messages that their value is based on their performance.

In my story from chapter 3, many of my false visceral beliefs stemmed from a lack of sufficient emotional connection and direction in childhood. In Anisa's story, which she shares here, it was the opposite.

> I grew up in a middle-class family, went to a Christian school, and attended church. I received lots of parental attention and affection and suffered no significant loss or disappointment. All my needs and most of my wants were provided for.
>
> In school, I worked hard and got good grades. Honestly, if you could dream of a childhood where you felt safe, loved, and that you could accomplish anything you set your mind to, it's pretty close to what I lived.
>
> My parents taught me to pray and trust God and, because things generally seemed to come easily to me and work favorably for me, I carried into adulthood a belief that all I needed was prayer, faith, and a little hard work, and life would all work out.

Then came marriage and responsibilities. Then the disillusioning discovery in my mid-twenties that life doesn't, in fact, magically work itself out just because you pray and work hard. Not being able to reconcile the God of my childhood with my adult experience, I began shutting down my heart, operating subconsciously from a growing belief that God didn't truly love me, see me, or care about me. The girl who'd prayed so openly and trustingly for God to give her an undivided heart slowly became the woman so disconnected from her heart that she wouldn't even acknowledge her longing for a pair of colorful socks.

Anisa's painful journey toward a shutdown, disconnected heart is far more common and pervasive than most people realize. Over the last twenty-one years of leading teams through the Battle for the Heart process, we've walked with thousands of men and women, most of whom are committed Christians and leaders in their churches. Most know a significant amount of biblical truth about God and themselves.

So, I was puzzled when I first started hearing from many of those leaders, including pastors, that their primary takeaway from their experience was: "God loves me." Many were discovering that God not only loves them but actually likes them!

"Wait, how can that be?" I wondered. "That's Bible 101!"

But then I began to realize that much of their biblical knowledge kept bouncing off closed hearts. They had the beautiful theology of the first half of Ephesians in which Paul paints a captivating picture of God's love that redeems, restores, and connects us to Christ and one another, bridging the divide between Jew and Gentile. Those leaders knew and understood Paul's challenge in the second half of Ephesians to live out that glorious picture in the trenches of a diverse church overcoming racial, ethnic, and socioeconomic divisions. They knew his call to sacrificially love in countercultural ways in the context of marriage and family. What they lacked, though, was a depth of personal, experiential knowing of the Father's love for them as unique human beings whom he likes and delights in, not just tolerates because of Christ in them. This knowing brings security, peace, and freedom to love as we have been loved.

Paul understood from his own experience that it takes not just a captivating vision but a captivating experience of divine love to break down the walls of fear and pride within us and among us. So, Paul prays that this diverse community of believers would be "rooted and grounded" in the love of Christ so that together they may experientially know his love that transcends knowledge and fills them with the fullness of God. This empowers them to fulfill the commands of the rest of Ephesians (see 3:17–21; 4:32–5:2 ESV).

In an agriculturally oriented society, those believers would understand that a plant can only flourish when its roots extend deep into good soil. Similarly, we grow as we are rooted in the good soil that is God's love.

But what happens when the roots hit dams of concrete covering up shut-down and wounded hearts or protective strategies designed to shield us from pain or gain the pleasure we seek? That's where Paul uses a construction analogy. He prays that we will be grounded or established in the love of Christ. This term refers to the foundation of a building. The only solid foundation that will withstand the storms of life and guide us to answering the deepest questions of our hearts is the sacrificial, steadfast love of God in Christ. That foundation is only built as we increasingly open our whole hearts to the love of Christ permeating our hearts.

So, what must the Divine Builder do to clear out the concrete dams in our hearts blocking the love of God from permeating our hearts? Blow them up.

Dam Demolition

God in his goodness, in his love for you and me, longs to blow up the dams in our lives so that we may experience the exhilarating grace of a wild, bountiful, free-flowing river of divine life in and through the wellspring of our hearts (see John 7:37–38 ESV)!

That is the good news. However, the only way to blow up a dam as large and well built as the Hoover Dam is with lots of explosives. These explosives often come in the form of trials and suffering.

> Consider it pure joy, my brothers and sisters, whenever you face trials of many kinds, because you know that the testing of your faith produces perseverance. Let perseverance finish its work so that you may be mature and complete, not lacking anything. (James 1:2–4)

Trials and suffering can come from different sources. They can come from our own false beliefs, from simply living in a broken world, or because of the persecution that comes as we live out our faith in a hostile world. They often involve relationships, particularly those important to us. Regardless of their cause, trials and suffering come to all of us to test our faith and reveal what is true about our hearts. Trials and suffering point us to the One who sees us and who is present no matter how deep the pain or the pit; the One who holds us in his hands; the One who longs for us to become "mature and complete" in him.

These places of trial and suffering, these places of deep pain, hold the greatest potential for transformation. In the vulnerability of suffering, we have a choice: Do we hold onto the familiar and reach for the armor to reinforce the faulty foundation of pride and self-protective strategies? Or do we, like David, clothe ourselves with humility, act with naked and bold trust, and refuse man-made armor that keeps us from living in the fullness of life with God?

From the time God used a sister to reveal a simple picture of the Hoover Dam to me and I prayed a dangerous prayer, he carefully took nineteen months to root me deeper in his steadfast, loving goodness, particularly through meditating in Psalm 139.

Five months in, God, in a most unusual way, guided me to the story of Hagar, the Egyptian slave of Sarah, the barren wife of Abraham. After Hagar becomes pregnant with Abraham's child, Sarah mistreats her, and Hagar flees. The angel of the LORD comes to her by a wellspring in the desert. After their personal interchange, Hagar "names the LORD who spoke to her, 'You are the God who sees me'" (Genesis 16:13).

That night as I reflected on how God led me to this story and on the story itself, I saw the "God who sees me." I knew God was coming after me. He wanted me to deeply know that HE sees me and he knows ME even when it feels like I'm dying in the desert.

Months later, when the trial and pain came, it did so in a way and a depth I could never have imagined . . .

It came at my favorite time of year—the Christmas season, December 2001. It's the time when Mary and I find a beautiful live tree, decorate it, enjoy the evergreen aroma, sit by a warm fire, and celebrate Immanuel, God with us. The week before Christmas, I experienced a series of relational explosions from several couples close to me. They were couples I had poured my life into for decades. As the first explosion hit on a Tuesday afternoon, I found it hard to believe that a relationship I'd given so much to now felt at risk. How could this be? I felt misunderstood, unappreciated, and not valued. Surely, we could work things out. Then came the second explosion. Then the third. Now the pain turned into a sense of betrayal. It seemed incomprehensible.

Thursday, I reached out to a pastor friend who had himself navigated relational explosions. I shared with him my confidence that things would work out. He wasn't so sure.

Friday, I sat in my study at home on the phone with one of the husbands. I longed for resolution and reconnection. After a few moments of talking, I said with growing desperation, "We've got to meet."

He agreed, then said, "I'm leaving town, but we can meet Monday, on Christmas Eve." Ten days away. Ten days of waiting, without resolution.

We closed the conversation, and unlike most other conversations we'd had, he hung up without any words of affirmation or connection. He gave no assurance that this would work out.

In that moment, my hopes of reconnection and resolution evaporated. I felt a pain so deep that for the first time in my life, I could identify with an alcoholic who has been sober for years but, because the pain is so great, he reaches for a bottle to deaden the pain. In that moment, it hit me that my drug of choice, my North Star—achievement that promised connection, value, and significance—had deceived me.

In the searing pain of betrayal my North Star lay shattered around me. My protective strategies had catastrophically failed.

In the pain, I finally looked up and cried out to God, "You *have* to help me."

In that moment, I heard him whisper to me, "You are my son whom I love, in whom I am well pleased."

I recognized the message. God had been repeating it to me throughout the year. So, I responded, *"That's not good enough. I need something more."*

And then he whispered back to me in words I'll never forget: "That's as good as it gets."

Becoming Larry the Beloved

In the pain of these exploding relationships, I now faced an existential question, a question I had been subconsciously asking from the earliest moments of my life, but I had never fully faced: Am I truly loved?

Sitting in the middle of shattered expectations and searing rejection, could I believe in the depths of my heart that God loved me and that he was pleased with me?

Could I dare believe in radical grace, in sheer unmerited favor? I knew all about it at a rational level, but in the depth of all the pain I felt, it was counterintuitive to the foundation of performance-based achievement I had, at a visceral level, built my whole life upon.

Yet, somehow, in the utter, naked vulnerability of that moment, what I rationally believed to be true—what I longed to believe—broke through the concrete shell around my heart and became experiential truth in the deepest, hidden parts of my heart.

I finally whispered back to God with a deep sense of rest: *"Yes, I am your beloved son. Yes, I believe you are pleased with me."*

A peace I had not felt in a long time washed over me. I had been waking up in the middle of the night with fear and anxiety, but that night I woke up with a sense of being covered in a canopy of divine love, pleasure, and protection. I then went back to sleep.

The next morning, I woke up a changed man and have never struggled in this way since.

Just kidding! ☹

Looking back, that experience became a defining point in my life—a catalyst for change—but it took me years before I really understood what happened that day. In searing pain, I experienced God's love detonating the concrete around my heart in order to free the roots of his love to grow deep into the soil of my whole heart.

I'd had a taste of Jesus' promise "Blessed are those who mourn for they shall be comforted" (Matthew 5:4). *Blessed* speaks of the fullness of shalom, of divine peace that is a taste of Eden.

We can only experience the fullness we long for, we can only be all we were created to be, as we let go of what is fallen and false and take hold of that which is true. In the letting go there is often pain, loss, and mourning that opens our hearts to take hold of the comfort of knowing the Father's presence, love, and even delight.

On that day, the Divine Builder struck a major blow in the fallen, false foundation of Larry the Achiever and laid a major stone to restore the true foundation of Larry the Beloved.

The flawed foundation of Larry the Achiever took forty-eight years to build, piece by piece, most of it subconsciously and some consciously through choices I made. As I experienced God shattering major pieces of that foundation, as I chose to believe his love, grace, and truth speaking to my deepest questions of "Am I loved?" and "Who am I?" something amazing began to happen, something I didn't even realize. The Divine Builder was bringing forth the *true* foundation of Larry the Beloved. The foundation laid the moment he created me for glory and honor. The foundation that fell from glory and honor in the fall of Adam and Eve. The foundation he came to redeem when, as a fifteen-year-old, I trusted Christ as my Lord and Savior.

This momentous experience began an ongoing shift that ultimately culminated in the profound realization that as I deeply know God's love, my very identity becomes Larry the Beloved. This identity energizes my purpose to reveal God's glory, his love, grace and truth through the unique person he has created me to be.

Evil came to distort who I uniquely am through the fall and the false foundations or dams I built. Christ came to redeem God's creative work in me that I might do the good works he prepared for me (see Ephesians 2:9–10). But like Michaelangelo chiseling on a flawed piece of marble to bring forth David, God keeps chiseling off the remnants of Larry the Achiever to bring forth Larry the Beloved.

As God does his chiseling, mini-explosions continue and new insights into my distorted thinking arise, but I am moving toward believing more fully the familiar words of my Heavenly Father: "You are my son, whom I love, in whom I am well pleased."

That is as good as it gets, now and for all eternity.

FOR DEEPER CONNECTION

Personalize

How do you relate to the concept of having internal blockages that keep you from experiencing God's love and becoming who you're created to be?

Gain Awareness

What impact has your experience of love in human relationships had on the way you experience God's love?

All of us carry some degree of internal blockage that keeps us from fully experiencing God's love. This limits our capacity to express his love to others. What gain would make it worth the potential pain of opening your heart to God and allowing him to blow up the dams in your heart that it might become a more freely flowing wellspring?

Respond

As you feel led, share with God about the places where you struggle to trust his heart and the change you long for in your relationship with him.

CHAPTER 6

"I Will Come to You"

Connecting to the God who loves you and likes you

Anisa

"I will not leave you as orphans; I will come to you."
John 14:18

I will come to you . . .

They are words that resound from creation into eternity. They're the Father, first coming to us in Eden and hand-fashioning man from dust and woman from man. Then, in intimate connection, breathing his very breath into their lungs (see Genesis 2:7). They are words that echo through the ages in increasing volume as if with every step we take, every fall, every scrape, God's voice speaks: "I will come to you."

I imagine these words carried on a breeze to Adam and Eve in the face of their brokenness. When two who knew no shame first tasted its bitter brew. When innocent eyes first opened to sin and the weight of it crashed like a tide upon them. When the gulf between what was meant to be and what now is seemed unfathomable.

But God came near and called them out of hiding. He shed an animal's blood to clothe them and cover their sin and shame.

"I will come to you . . ."

Now whispered to Noah when sin permeated the human race. God's grief was deep at the inclinations of the human heart. His first thought was to blot out his created beings (vv. 6:5–7), but he looked among the many to find one. To that one, God came. For that one and his family, God made a way.

"I will come to you..."

Spoken louder yet to Abraham when God called unto himself a people who would be a blessing to the nations (see Genesis 12:3)—then to Isaac and Jacob with whom he confirmed his promise. "I will be your God, and you will be my people"—a refrain that echoes throughout the Story all the way to Consummation (see Genesis 17:7; Exodus 6:7; Jeremiah 7:23; Revelation 21:3).

"I will come to you..."

Louder still to Moses when God's people, after 400 years of captivity, cried out. Their backs were breaking; their hope was waning. Then God sent a deliverer, Moses, to lead his people out of bondage into the fullness of the promised land (see Exodus 3).

"I will come to you..."

In heartrending ways, the voice of God came through the prophets as he persistently, tenderly, passionately called a wayward bride back to be his beloved.

"I will come to you..."

Immanuel, meaning "God with us," came as a human baby who would open himself to take all the pain, all the suffering, and all the sin of the world; as one who would shed his blood to close the unfathomable gulf between us and himself to eternally reconnect us to the Father. This is the heart of the gospel message. God came in creation. He came in redemption. And he is coming again. Then he will be our God, and we will be his people.

Love That Transforms

"I will not leave you as orphans; I will come to you."

With these simple words Jesus captures the essence of God's Larger Story: God created us for connection with himself, and he is not content to leave us in our broken, disconnected state. He has and always will come for us, his orphaned children.

If you can, imagine yourself among the pages of scripture, your story illustrating God's pursuit. How have you experienced God coming to you? How have you responded?

When you look back at just the fraction of stories captured in scripture that tell of God's love, it's astounding. Over and over, he lays his heart bare. He tells of his unending desire to be our God, and for us to be his people. He loves people who fail to love him back. He's faithful to the faithless. It's easy to hold these ancient stories at a distance, to wonder at the apparent blindness of the children of Israel. God endlessly provided incredible miracles, yet they still struggled to trust him.

It would be easy to say, "How could they *not* trust him?" But are we any different? Are there not times when we all feel and act as if we are orphaned, abandoned by our loving Father? Why is this? Because each of us harbor places in our hearts that God's love has not fully touched.

As mentioned previously, it is not enough to know God's love intellectually. For transformation, we must know it experientially. Experiential knowing is wholehearted knowing. It is an integration of the heart—our desires, feelings, thoughts, and choices—that comes as we are rooted and grounded in God's love, grace, and truth (see Ephesians 3:17–19).

When we find ourselves stuck, struggling to grow spiritually, struggling to overcome sin, it is often an indicator that there are disconnections between our stated beliefs about God's love and our visceral knowing of God's love. Author and psychologist David Benner in his book *Surrender to Love* says, "Ultimately, problems in surrender and obedience are problems of knowing God's love."[8]

How so? As mentioned in chapter 2, Evil seeks to disrupt our intimacy with God so our capacity to reveal his character is diminished. When we lack intimate connection with God, we live from a distorted sense of identity and purpose since both our identity—a beloved image bearer—and our purpose—to love as we have been loved—flow from our experience of intimacy. We saw this in Larry's story when, out of a lack of emotional connection, direction, and protection, he looked to achievement to get the connection and significance he longed for. He failed to live in the truth that his very identity is that of a beloved image bearer, thus sabotaging his deep desire to be loved and to fulfill his desire and purpose to love.

God longs to answer your deep heart questions, so he actively pursues you to draw you to himself and into a deeper experience of his love. Your part is to simply respond with surrender, opening your whole heart to his love. This lifelong journey of increasingly knowing God's love is what brings change that goes beyond behavior modification to the whole heart transformation only God can accomplish in us.

When we know God's love in our whole heart, our heart is changed so we increasingly desire and choose what God desires. As Benner says, obedience "grows out of soaking myself in this love so thoroughly that love for God springs up in response."[9]

Surrender to God's love is the work of his Spirit, making his love ours and his nature ours. This is the core of Christian spiritual transformation.

Intimacy energizes purpose. The more we experience God's love at a whole-heart level, the more we will be transformed and enabled to love as God loves. This is beautifully illustrated in Bob's story.

A Wholehearted Experience of Love

Bob is a highly relational leader who was the founding pastor of a thriving congregation of about twenty-five hundred when he attended his first Battle for the Heart retreat in 2009.

Bob found Christ while in college at Penn State University, and upon graduation spent three years serving with a campus ministry before planting a church in a growing area of Birmingham, Alabama.

But underneath all the outward signs of success, Bob struggled with significant anxiety. He was always striving—to get things right, to live up to others' expectations, to measure up—and, deep down, believed that he only had worth or value when he lived up to those expectations. Though he often experienced outward success, the pressure to perform was always there. His fear of failure was overwhelming.

The seeds of anxiety were sown in Bob's childhood. In the shadow of the Vietnam War, images of the unfolding crisis flooded his family's television every evening—images he couldn't help but absorb. Bob recalls, "I cried myself to sleep every night thinking 'I'm going to have to go to war. I don't want to fight. I'm afraid. I'm just a little boy.'"

Bob also lived in the time of, and near the serial killer, the Boston Strangler. Then he walked through a traumatic hospital experience where he was strapped down and powerless. These experiences contributed to a growing visceral belief that the world was not safe.

Parents and authority figures didn't know how to help Bob navigate his fears, so they encouraged him to try harder to move beyond it or to toughen up. For Bob, the world was a scary place, and without the tools or support he needed to work through his fears, he internalized a subconscious message: *I've got to control my world. It's up to me to figure out everything that can go wrong in order to avoid pain and guarantee success.*

During middle and high school sports, Bob excelled at athletics, touching his deep unrecognized desires for relational connection and being part of something bigger than himself. But sports also became another avenue of pain. At one point, he recalls being a well-liked running back on the junior high school football team when, for no apparent reason, other team members turned on him, writing violent messages about him and shunning him for months. The same was repeated in Bob's life in senior high basketball. While Bob was skilled and successful, friends and teammates shunned him unexpectedly and without explanation.

As a confused boy, he didn't understand why people he thought were friends one day turned on him the next. Life again felt unsafe, dangerous. And again, the subconscious message he received was *"It's up to me. It's up to me to keep myself safe from pain. It's up to me to make people like me so I won't be rejected."*

In his sophomore year of college, Bob came to know Christ. His desire to impact others by sharing with them the grace that had so impacted him led him to vocational ministry. His gifts of communication and connecting with others made him an extremely effective and well-liked pastor. He found significant satisfaction knowing he was living in God's will for his life.

Despite being a gifted and effective leader, Bob still had battle scars. The creative, imaginative child grew to be a creatively gifted teacher who still felt the need for control, to think through everything that could potentially go wrong, keep it from going wrong, and protect himself from harm. The team player grew to be a team builder, impacting thousands nationally and internationally, yet he still carried fears of rejection and lived with high level, but hidden, internal anxiety.

Instead of being able to rest in God's pleasure as he played his part in God's Larger Story, Bob was constantly striving. Those childhood wounds and messages led to areas of internal heart disconnection which blocked Bob from fully experiencing God's love and delight in him. His fear-based response—to control people and situations—drained others and made them feel like something was wrong with them. This diminished his capacity to fulfill his purpose, to love as he was loved. Longing for more, Bob continued to pursue God even as God pursued him. "I will come to you . . ."

At Bob's first Battle for the Heart retreat Larry shared his painful journey as Larry the Achiever, of discovering the disconnection between what he rationally and viscerally believed about God's love. Larry explained how the disconnection began to close when he realized that the heart of God's Larger Story is his initiating, pursuing love.

As Bob listened, God opened his eyes to see more clearly an eternal perspective of the Larger Story that began long before his story and would continue long afterward. Bob shared:

> Thinking through the Larger Story blew me away. God's Larger Story is like a flowing stream involving billions of people over thousands of years, and each one of us has a significant part in the stream of that Story. Our contribution continues the contribution of people who have gone before us and impacts those downstream.
>
> I guess I just never thought of it that way before. It's simultaneously huge and incredibly humbling. It's huge in that I can't believe I get the privilege of playing a part in a story this large. Yet it's humbling in that I'm simply one drop in this eternal ever-flowing stream of God's Larger Story.

As Bob responded to God's pursuit by opening his whole heart, his heart became more fully integrated. The biblical truth he rationally believed and tried to live from became a more visceral truth that he could act and react from. As he recognized the lie that everything was up to him, he began to relax and let go of the need to control and to perform. He was beginning to experience the love that surpasses knowledge.

Let's break down what this process looked like based on more specifics in his story.

What was Bob thinking? As Bob saw the captivating, huge, humbling beauty of the Larger Story and his part in it, his *rational* knowledge of the biblical truth of God's divine love broke through to *visceral* belief. His thinking began to shift from "It's all up to me to keep myself safe" to trusting in God's love and goodness regardless of his circumstances.

What was Bob feeling and desiring? His *felt* experience of God's pursuing love touched his deep *desires* to be loved, protected, and cared for. This began to dissipate his anxiety, increasingly releasing him from intensity and the need to perform.

What was Bob choosing? This deeper knowing of truth increasingly freed Bob to let go of control and be okay to simply live his part in the stream of God's Larger Story.

As Bob let go of fear-driven control and intensity, he was able to love more effectively and to increasingly live from his true identity and purpose. People who had once felt drained by Bob's controlling behavior experienced being built up in love and found increasing freedom to grow in their own identity and purpose.

Encountering a Wholehearted God

In working through the almost yearlong Battle for the Heart process, Bob discovered how to engage God in the scriptures with all four levels of his heart. Returning a year later with another group from his church, Bob began to see in scripture that God, too, is wholehearted. This challenged his perceptions of how God saw and related to him.

Never in his wildest dreams, Bob recalls, could he have imagined that God had feelings for him or that God could have a *deep desire* to love and pursue him.

This growing awareness began to settle a frustration stemming from Bob's think-do approach to connecting with God and scripture.

> I longed for more in my relationship with God. I wanted to know him better and experience him more, but all I knew to do was to read the Bible more. I didn't understand what the deficit could

be. So, I began to think there was something wrong with me. In my think-do category there was nothing more to do except try harder. I needed to know more Scripture, think about more Scripture, process more Scripture, and then just apply it better. It led to me trying harder and hoping that something would change. But all it led to was more frustration. Either I was a screwup or God was displeased with me, and I didn't know why.

As Bob continued growing in his wholehearted approach to God, his experience of scripture changed. In passage after passage, story after story, his old view of God as a "brain on a stick" who thought about him and chose to love him but had no feelings toward or desires about him, began to shift. Bob began to see and intimately know a God who *desired* to love him, who *felt* love toward him, and who actually liked him—a God who *grieved* when Bob didn't trust him but always desired to come to him and comfort him in his pain and fear.

As Bob continued to surrender to this deeper knowing of a wholehearted God, the grace Bob so powerfully communicated to thousands of others began to detonate the false messages in his own heart: he was *not* a screwup, and God was *not* displeased with him! Bob began experiencing God's joy and delight in him, even in his mistakes. Bob's view of himself and his sense of identity shifted to increasingly becoming God's beloved son who can relax and love. This empowered him to lead God's people into a more intimate experience of a wholehearted God who pursues them in love.

Rather than looking to people to validate him, Bob began to believe in and rest in God's validating voice. Bob began to have great hope in his worth and value of simply being a beloved son. He wasn't "fixed" or "healed", but he was in the stream of God's love while playing the part God created him to play. That brought joy and fulfillment to his heart, to those around him, and to the One who came to him.

Opening Our Hearts to Receive God's Love

In Bob's story we see a life transformed by a deeper knowing of God's love. Apart from our basic survival needs, the desires to love and be loved are among the most foundational needs and longings we have as humans. God created us out of love, to be loved, to experience his love, and to express his love. Yet we often struggle to believe in the deepest parts of our hearts that we are loved. Our self-protective strategies, our awareness of our fallen nature, and the actions of others who were supposed to love us but failed make it hard for us to open our hearts to receive love and to live as ones who are loved. But as John points out, it is in receiving God's love that we are empowered to love (I John 4:19).

Although we have tried to present in a simplified manner the concept of knowing God's love and increasing awareness about our need for a wholehearted knowing of love, that does not mean it is simple in practice. For many of us it's a struggle. Our ability to receive love and trust our hearts to God and others is impacted by our previous experience of love, particularly in our formative years. But we hope that you, like Bob, will increasingly know that God is pursuing you in love, that you might experience his love and be empowered to express his love.

So, how do we recognize the ways in which God demonstrates love, how he comes to us today?

We experience God's love,

- in connection with God—through a simple awareness of his presence. He speaks directly to us through words or impressions and through scripture and experiences such as ones we are sharing in this book;
- in community with others—as we serve as a channel of God's love and his pursuit. We'll talk more about love in community in the next chapter.

Experiencing God's Love Through Everyday Opportunities for Connection

We all have different ways of connecting to God. For some, it's through acts of service or caregiving, participating in worship, creating something beautiful like art or music, or seeking out silence and solitude for contemplation. How you connect with God is not as important as simply making space to do it, then opening your whole heart to let his presence—his love, grace, and truth—fill your desires, affect your feelings, captivate your thoughts, and motivate your choices.

For me, God speaks significantly through creation, so when I take a walk or sit outside and soak in the beauty of nature, I try to be attentive to what God is doing inside my heart. Where do I feel connected to or distant from him? How am I experiencing his love in the moment? What feelings and desires are being touched? What choice, if any, is God leading me to make? If I don't start my time with scripture, I try to end with it, assessing everything I sense God speaking to me through the lens of scripture.

Experiencing God's Love Through Scripture

God's Word is a love story, and love isn't distant. It is up close and personal. So, our approach to scripture needs to be up close and personal. We must read it and, ultimately, let it read us. Let it search our hearts so we can understand the true state of our inner being (see Psalm 139; Jeremiah 17:7–10).

As we read scripture, we need to interact with it, creating space for it to impact us at all four levels of our heart. Bob illustrates this below in a recent personal reflection using the "Engaging with Scripture from the Four Levels of the Heart" template located in the back of this book and downloadable at becomingwholehearted.org.

> The LORD your God is in your midst,
>   a mighty one who will save;
> he will rejoice over you with gladness;
>   he will quiet you by his love;
> he will exult over you with loud singing.
> (Zephaniah 3:17 ESV)

Thinking level: What do I think about this passage? How does it potentially apply to my life? How have I experienced this truth? In what ways does this seem not to match my current experience of life?

> Rationally, I know these are true statements about God and statements of God's promises toward his people. But I find myself asking the question: When are these statements true in my own experience? I still am so quick to head toward a transactional view of my relationship with God, defaulting to the thoughts that his posture toward me is based on how well I'm performing in the Christian life. Yet, over time I have learned to more quickly say, like David, "Soul, put your hope in God!" (Psalm 42:5, 11; 43:5). It is still a battle for me, but by coming to rely upon God's love, I am more quickly aware of the lies I'm tempted to believe.

Feeling level: How do I feel about this passage? How do I feel as I consider the ways I have experienced this truth? How do I feel as I struggle to reconcile this truth with my current experience of life?

> I sometimes feel conflicted as I read this verse because, at times, it still doesn't seem to match my own experience of the Christian life. Yet I also experience the truth of God's love for me rapturously, even ecstatically at other times. Then there are times I still experience the fear that these verses are true of others but only *maybe* true of me. I'm afraid I'll just never viscerally experience the beauty of this verse consistently.

But God is cupping my face in his hands in fresh ways and turning my gaze upon Jesus—the One who has given me the standing of the beloved before the Father—and as a result, I am resting more confidently and more often in the reality of this passage. I am filled with gratitude and joy and hope as a result.

Desires level: What do I long for as I read this passage? What deep desires in me are being met as I receive this truth? What deep desires are not being met as I live in this place where God's truth is not yet fully realized in my life?

> This passage touches upon a deep desire to experience connectedness and intimacy with the Triune God . . . to experience his love for me at a wholehearted level. I long to hear his "Well done!" and I deeply desire to experience his delight in me. As I come to rely upon His love for me expressed in this passage, these deep desires are being met in him.

Choosing: What choices do I want to make as I consider this passage? Try to identify choices that flow from your deep desires and move you toward connection with God and others. Seek to be honest with God about areas where you're struggling.

> I choose to believe this verse is true for one reason and one reason only: Zephaniah 3:17 was purchased for me and every believer in Jesus Christ by his finished work, and its truth is not dependent upon my performance. I choose to believe I am a beloved, adopted child, as loved by God as the eternal Son is loved. I choose to continue to surrender any lingering pain from the past and trust that, as I surrender to love within the scope of faith, my new experiences will increasingly match my faith in Christ. I am learning that as I choose to rely upon the Father's love expressed in this passage and choose to believe, because of my union with Christ, it's true for me *all* the time I am more consistently experiencing his

love. God continues to replace old roots of fear and unbelief with new roots grounded in his love.

Replacing "old roots of fear and unbelief with new roots grounded in his love"—that's what leads to lasting spiritual transformation. As Bob's combined story and reflection illustrate, this is an ongoing, deepening journey into the heart of God, a God who so deeply cares for you, he will not leave you orphaned, cut off from his love. He comes to you in joy and in sorrow. And when you feel yourself slipping or struggling to connect with a God who is near yet sometimes seems far away, he longs to surround you with a community of his people to serve as channels of that love.

It is to this community aspect of love that we now direct our attention.

FOR DEEPER CONNECTION

Personalize

As you consider the difference between knowing God's love intellectually and knowing God's love experientially, what do you realize about the way you connect or struggle to connect to God's love?

Gain Awareness

Identify two or three feeling words that capture what is going on in your heart as you consider your response to the previous question. (See the Feelings chart in the Toolbox.)

If you could live more fully from the truth of God's love—so it touches your thoughts, feelings, and choices—what deep desires in you would that meet? (See Desires chart in Toolbox.)

Respond

Father, help me open my heart more fully to the experience of your love. Show me the ways that even today you are pursuing me in love to demonstrate you care for me.

CHAPTER 7

I Will Come to You in Community

Opening your heart to love and be loved in community

Larry

In eighth grade I was secretary of our student council—by ninth grade I was president. I loved politics, not just at school, but also at state and national levels. I watched the presidential nominating conventions and loved the challenges and debates around important issues. Through it all, I dreamed of being president of the United States.

I vividly remember the most famous Army commercial in US history: "Be all you can be." I didn't really want to go into the Army, but the message connected to something deep within that I didn't even realize as a teenager.

Looking back, I now see the thread of deep desires connecting all these experiences: to be all I could be, to be part of something larger than myself, and to do it together with people committed to the same vision!

Why do stories of battle, heroism, love, duty, and being part of something larger—something good and noble—captivate our hearts? Because they are echoes of God's Larger Story that resound within us. As the writer of Ecclesiastes describes it, "He has made everything beautiful in its time. He has also set eternity in the human heart; yet no one can fathom what God has done from beginning to end" (v. 3:11).

Great stories draw us into the Larger Story where for a fleeting moment we taste eternity. They touch deep desires that can only be fully satisfied in God and his Larger Story.

As people of God, created by the community of the Trinity, we find and fulfill our purpose as we live connected to God in community with others. God has uniquely crafted each of us and entrusted us with specific spheres of influence at work, at home, in church, and in our communities. Within these spheres, we have the honor of representing God.

We saw in the last chapter that at the heart of the Larger Story is God's pursuing love. Everything God does flows out of love. But his love has many expressions. He is gracious and compassionate (see Isaiah 30:18). He is a fierce warrior (see Jeremiah 20:11) who administers justice (see Isaiah 42:1–4). He defends the orphans, widows, and foreigners (see Deuteronomy 10:18). He loves so deeply, so sacrificially, that he gave his only Son that whoever believes in him may have eternal life (see John 3:16).

Since our love flows from God's love, our love also has many expressions. We love as we fight for the hearts of others. We do this by extending kindness to strangers, forgiving those who have wronged us, protecting the defenseless, administering justice and pursuing peace, faithfully serving in our jobs, training our children in godliness, and stewarding our homes and the earth's resources.

Your purpose, your part in God's Larger Story, is not dependent on you having a specific job, role, or responsibilities. It doesn't require you to be single or married. Your purpose is the same whether you're at home, work, or the check-out line at the grocery store. You are called to simply be an expression of God's character, his love wherever you are, whatever you are doing (see Colossians 3:17).

This is our personal and shared mission and the essence of wholehearted community—wholehearted believers coming together to experience and express God's love to him, one another, and the world.

To play our part in God's Larger Story, to live as the Body of Christ in community overflowing with God's love, we must choose the Way of Humility.

Figure 7.0

The Way of Humility	
Surrender	to divine love
Open	your whole heart to love in community
Embrace	God in suffering, trusting his goodness
Trust	God's promises to bring resurrection, life, and glory in his time and way
Energy: love, grace, and truth	
Result: connection, intimacy	

As we saw through Bob's story, playing our part in God's story depends on the depth to which we experience his love. This is why the Way of Humility begins with the choice to surrender to love. Surrender, in this context, means entrusting ourselves to God's love—yielding our independence and relying on the redeeming work of Christ.

Experiencing God's love then gives us courage to open our whole, authentic, vulnerable hearts to love in community.

Experiencing God's Love in Community with Others

Why do we need courage to open ourselves to love in community? Because we are fallen image bearers in the process of being restored who don't always love well. And we are wounded by other fallen image bearers who fail to love us well. In the brokenness of our relationships, Evil tempts us to inappropriately self-protect our hearts, to withdraw from others, and choose the Way of Pride which leads to disconnection.

To open our hearts to others involves risk, as Anisa shares . . .

> In my journey toward becoming wholehearted, opening my heart to deeper connection and dependence on God seemed easier than opening myself to others. I knew there would be times others would let me down. To live in authentic, vulnerable relationships felt risky and unsafe. And I felt like depending on others made me an unwanted burden. But as I began opening myself more vulnerably to others and acknowledging my need for them, I began to glimpse something of God's plan for community—how we are intended to know his love more fully as we live together with other believers (see Ephesians 3:14–19). I realized that while my self-protective strategies might spare me some pain, they also kept me from the joy of connection with those God placed in my life as a channel of his love, grace, and truth to me.
>
> For example, when someone sends a text checking up on me after I've had a hard week, I feel seen, cared for, not alone, and I'm actually giving others the opportunity to be who they are created to be by allowing myself to be loved in community.
>
> This was a huge paradigm shift for me: I cannot be who I am created to be unless I not only open my heart *to love* others but open my heart to *be loved* by others. Knowing this energizes me to risk living in community even knowing at times it will be messy and painful.

How are we called to love in community? To truly love as God loves is to choose, even sacrificially, for the good of others. As the apostle John says, "This is how we know what love is: Jesus Christ laid down his life for us. And we ought to lay down our lives for our brothers and sisters" (1 John 3:16).

We cannot know, perfectly, what is in the best interest of others, so to love this way requires courage and humility. It requires courage to risk opening our hearts to others to both offer love, knowing they might reject our offering, and to receive love from those who want to sacrificially love us! It requires humility as we live connected to the Trinity, God's Word, and other believers who are willing to speak the truth in love.

When we sacrificially love, we protect and propel others into their part in the Larger Story. We protect as we battle for the hearts of one another by revealing God's heart. We can do that in a multitude of ways including by simply being present, carrying one another's burdens, practicing hospitality, rejoicing with those who rejoice and mourning with those who mourn, and speaking the truth in love so that together we may all grow to become the mature body of Christ overflowing with the love of God (see Galatians 6:2; Romans 12:13–15; Ephesians 4:15–16).

We propel as we "spur one another on toward love and good deeds" that display God's glory (Hebrews 10:24). We do this as we share with others, in humility, the glory of God we see in them as well as any distortions or self-protective strategies that we see blocking the flow of that glory through the wellspring of their hearts. These gentle spurs can be hard to give and to receive. But as we'll see in my graduate school story, the impact can be significant.

Community That Protects and Propels

Back in May 2000, in response to the woman who saw a dam hindering God's spirit in me, I prayed a reluctant prayer for God to reveal anything blocking the flow of his Spirit through the wellspring of my heart. Then God, in his kindness, kept coming to me, through his Spirit, scriptures, and the Body of Christ. This vital heart work prepared me for the devastating dam demolition of December 2001 where God tenderly whispered, "You are my son, whom I love, in whom I am well pleased."

As my trust in God's love grew, he guided Mary and me the following spring into a discernment process with our church elders about my vocational direction. Within months, we were at peace that God was leading us out of pastoral ministry, but to where, we did not know. We spent the rest of that year preparing the church and ourselves for the transition.

Later that year, God came to us through a week long experience designed to help us discover our unique part in God's Larger Story. We did this in a community of four other couples, two coaches, and a counselor. The intensity of preparation and the challenging yet encouraging feedback made for a rich process. God solidified my understanding of the particular way he created and crafted my life to express my purpose: guiding people into experiencing and expressing the depth and breadth of God's love.

A few months later, in spring 2003, God came to me through my experience of prayer and fasting in the North Georgia Mountains. There he continued the work of affirming my purpose as I began to see a vision for building a space for people to come and experience the depth of God's love within community, a vision that would become Wellspring Group.

As my vision developed, God knew that before I could build the space, there were more dams he had to detonate. I had to first experience his love, grace, and truth in the type of community he wanted me to build. So, he took me into the community of an intensive six-week graduate school program in Christian counseling with around ten students, mostly staying in dorms and eating meals together.

In school, we spent mornings in class and afternoons sharing critical elements of our lives and practicing relational skills foundational to counseling. Each day we wrote a reflection for our professor on what we experienced and how that affected us at all four levels of our hearts: our desires, feelings, thoughts, and choices.

As I wrote, I opened my heart to more trusting, radical, and vulnerable honesty than I'd ever done before. The next day we'd get the reflection back with insightful, incisive comments and questions. Often, they were uncomfortable spurs that took me even deeper into discovering God's heart and my own heart, laying the foundation to eventually see my distortion of Larry the Achiever.

Through all of this, God was once again orchestrating a divine demolition.

At the end of three weeks, we gathered in the morning and shared written feedback with each classmate. Then we gave verbal feedback to three others on how we experienced them during our time together. This was an opportunity to see ourselves through the eyes of others.

I'll never forget when it was my turn to receive my feedback. I still feel the pit in my stomach as I remember my classmates' words:

> "Larry, you act like you are here, but I don't sense you're really here, truly present, or truly caring."

> "Larry, it's like we're having a potluck, and you're supposed to bring the brownies. But instead, you bring the whole meal. Your intensity drives us away."

> "Larry, you need to relax. Stop doing and start being. I can handle the heat but not the humidity."

Then my professor tied their comments all together as she shared, "Larry, you are driven to understand because you want to 'get it right' so you'll be affirmed or recognized, which for you seems to equal connection and significance. Yet the intensity of that drive pushes people away instead of drawing them toward you."

As my classmates shared, I tried to take everything in, but I felt like I was in a daze. I didn't fully realize it at the time, but they were touching some of the deepest pain of my life. The pain continued to build through lunchtime, and when I got back to my room for a break, I knelt by my bed and exploded with pain-filled tears.

I was sabotaging what I longed for most: authentic, relational connection. But what was I to do? If I tried to understand and work hard to change, it would just compound the problem!

I felt like I had been found guilty of something terrible without being given any direction for improvement. It was like being back in my childhood and hearing the message "You are on your own to figure it out."

The afternoon lab wasn't any easier. I heard the lies of the enemy taking the feedback and twisting it. Evil told me I had messed up. It certainly felt like I had.

After lab, I talked to the brother who challenged me to relax. He had become a trusted friend, so I was willing to risk opening my heart to him. Sharing my internal struggles, I asked, "What can I do?"

"Nothing," he told me. "Larry, you have spent your entire life trying to figure out how to get your desires met. When that doesn't happen, you figure out what you did or didn't do right and correct it. You're like a skilled 747 pilot before and during takeoff who is constantly scanning what is going on. You're intensely involved. However, once the airplane reaches cruising altitude, the pilot relaxes and puts the plane on automatic pilot. Larry, unfortunately, you never relax and switch to automatic pilot.

"Trust yourself, trust us, and let it all hang out," he added. "Larry, we love and accept you whether you change or not. However, if you want to increase your impact upon us, then you have to discover how to just *be*—to accept that we like you, so just let go, relax, and let us enjoy who you really are."

Even though his words were like a foreign language to me, I could feel his love and acceptance in my vulnerability. That slowly began to break down the lifelong visceral belief that if I didn't get it right, if I didn't come through, I would be rejected and abandoned.

This community offered me an authentic, relational connection by sharing the hard truth of how they experienced me—my intensity had negatively affected them. They had not experienced me as fully present. Yet they didn't withdraw; they didn't reject me. They chose to be the Body of Christ seeking to love me. The spur of the feedback hurt, yet I believed love motivated them. Their love invited me to want more, to just *be*.

The invitation felt vulnerable, counterintuitive. Yet somehow, I knew that this was the path to truly becoming Larry the Beloved who walked in the way of love, just as Christ loved us (see Ephesians 5:1–2).

Through that weekend, my heavenly Father guided me into grieving the pain that led to my protective strategies. Then, in the grieving, to embrace his comfort, his grace, and his forgiveness.

In the following weeks, I trusted him to help me let go of the intensity I had held inside and discover how to simply be me, the one whom he loves and with whom he is well pleased. This was another step in walking out the truth I had heard more than a year earlier—in December 2001.

I slowed down to become more attentive to my heart. I began to sense when I was tempted to strive, to seek affirmation, to gain more understanding so I could do better and control what was happening. As I gained this new awareness, I repeatedly chose to repent, let go, and relax. I took faltering steps to become more vulnerable in lab, sharing what was really going on inside me instead of trying to manage it. I became less focused on getting things right, and I was able to be more sensitive and present to the hearts of others.

One night, as I was struggling with some homework, I began to wonder, *Why am I working so hard on this?* As I became aware of my internal messages of having to come through for myself, for my professors, and for God—and the belief that I had to always achieve at a high level—I chose to let go of the pressure to complete the homework and to just relax. The next day in lab, as several people spoke about the difficult assignment, I shared that I simply decided, "What the hell? I give up. If I don't get it right, I'm still loved!"

As I shared, everyone laughed and celebrated my repentance and growth.

As we came to the end of our second three-week intensive, several of us went out to dinner. The three people whose loving, hard feedback spurred me weeks earlier shared their joy of seeing me relax and let go. They liked what they experienced.

As I celebrated their affirmation, I rejoiced in not being desperate for it. That felt like authentic growth in being at peace with myself, God, and others.

In a loving, authentic community, God detonated another major piece of the concrete dam and placed another stone in the foundation of becoming all he created me to be, Larry the Beloved. Through this experience God was also equipping me to fulfill my purpose of guiding others into a transforming experience of divine love in community.

God's Image in Us Gives Us the Capacity to Fulfill Our Purpose

In the suffering of this experience, in what felt like devastating pain, I choose to stay surrendered and connected to my heart, God's heart, and the hearts of my classmates and professors. Trusting the love of the people around me enabled me to receive honest, humble feedback which spurred me on to relax and allow more of my true self, created in the image of God, to shine forth. There is no greater expression of God's glory!

It is the image of God in us that gives us the capacity to be loved, to love, and to display his glory. We saw this in the creation story in chapter 2. Four times in Genesis 1:26–28 we see God created human beings in his image, his likeness. This points to an intimate, loving relationship such as that between a parent and a child who bears something of the very essence of the parent. Then, twice we see God has entrusted the rule of the earth to us.

Dr. John Walton describes it this way:

> The image is a physical manifestation of divine (or royal) **essence** that bears the **function** of that which it represents; this gives the image-bearer the **capacity** to **reflect** the attributes (love, faithfulness, justice, wisdom, etc.) of the one represented and **act** on his behalf (emphasis mine).[10]

Notice the stunning claims of this definition. God intimately took something of himself, his essence, and placed it into human beings. What God creates us for, he equips us for. By creating us in his image we are, in some beautiful, mysterious way, like him. We can have a relationship with him. We can experience his love, respond to his love, and reveal his love as we act on his behalf.

What does it mean to have the essence of God within us? Essence speaks to the intrinsic nature of something—that which is essential to its being. Consider an acorn. The essential nature of an acorn is its "oakness." An acorn will grow into an oak tree, if it receives the water, sunlight, and good soil necessary for growth. There are approximately 600 varieties of oak trees, but all are oaks *in essence*.

Similarly, human beings, though unique, have the same essence. The essence God places into human beings is his glory. God's glory speaks of the outward radiance of his internal being. God's glory is who he is and what he does. "The essence of his glory is what the Hebrews called his steadfast love that expresses itself in extraordinary acts of self-giving."[11]

God's love may be expressed through justice, mercy, compassion, or anger, but every desire, feeling, thought, and action of God is loving. Since God placed something of his essence in you, your essence as a human being is to experience and express love in its various forms. This is who you are. This is what you do. How you express it is through the unique way God created and crafted your life. There is no one else who reveals God's glory like you, who can play your part in his Story.

In the creation account, we saw that Adam and Eve could only do what they were created to do as they lived in intimate dependence upon their Creator. The same is true for us as Jesus so clearly pictured in John 15:5: "I am the vine; you are the branches. If you remain in me and I in you, you will bear much fruit; apart from me you can do nothing."

Relax—It's Not All Up to You!

What does this mean for you? It means, as you've seen in both Bob's story and mine, you can relax. God is the author and initiator of the Larger Story. He is pursuing you in love so that you can experience his love. Your response is to surrender to his love. To *be* loved. To allow that love to permeate the deepest places within you, to close the disconnect between your rational and your visceral understanding of love. God is more interested in what he is doing *in* you than *through* you. As you increasingly experience his love, the expression of his love through your life is a natural overflow. This overflow is the fruit of the vine that comes from abiding in Christ.

Becoming who you were created to be is the ongoing process of dying to the Way of Pride and living in the Way of Humility. It's less about trying to become someone new and more about allowing God to strip away those parts that aren't the real you. It's less about learning how to express God's glory and more about letting go of those things that block the experience of God's glory to and through you. As you open your heart to increasingly experience love, grace, and truth in community, you become who you are meant to be—"God's handiwork, created in Christ Jesus to do good works which God prepared in advance for us to do" (Ephesians 2:10).

As I have imperfectly sought to walk in the Way of Humility, I have experienced God's love, grace, and truth crafting, shaping, chiseling me by his Spirit, through his Word and the body of Christ that I may become his "handiwork," revealing his glory and loving goodness through actions.

Through it all, God is satisfying the deep desires I didn't even recognize as a teenage boy. By his amazing grace I am slowly becoming all I can be, playing my part in a large, eternal love story and doing it with people who are committed to the same vision.

This experience of living intimately connected to God and one another and fulfilling our purpose as a divine image bearer is the fullness of life we long for. It is what Jesus redeemed us for and what God invites us into as we simply, faithfully surrender to his divine love in the Way of Humility. Why, then, do we not always experience this fullness? Because our deceptive desires often entice us to choose the Way of Pride, to seek to meet our needs and to fulfill our deepest desires independent of God. This is what we will explore next.

FOR DEEPER CONNECTION

Personalize

How do you connect with the desire to be part of something greater than yourself—a community, a cause, God's Larger Story?

Gain Awareness

What happens in your heart as you consider fully surrendering to divine love?

What deep desires are touched in you as you consider that God has chosen you for his Larger Story?

Respond

Heavenly Father, open my eyes to truly see the people you have placed in my life and the ways I can show your love, grace, and truth to them and receive the same from them.

CHAPTER 8

Desires That Deceive

How desires can sabotage what we long for

Anisa

"Larry, it's about the people, not the organization. God cares more about the people than the structure."

When Bryan spoke those words in a coffee shop years ago, they carried the weight of his journey to become the man and leader God created him to be.

"That conversation was significant for both of us. In many ways it was hard to say, hard to believe that in that moment God was more concerned about how we cared for the people. Whatever happened to the ministry was secondary."

A type-A, highly driven person, Bryan had spent two decades building a successful investment firm primarily serving large Christian ministries. What he didn't notice, though, was the collateral damage being left in his wake: the people.

Bryan knew biblical truth. He tried to love God and love others. Outwardly, he appeared to succeed. But one day at a spiritual conference, Bryan heard God speak to him about "having a form of godliness but denying its power" (2 Timothy 3:5).

"I left that event in tears, got in the car, called my pastor, and said, 'I've got to come in and see you.' I had this terrible feeling that I had missed the mark, both spiritually and holistically. My walk with Christ just wasn't what it seemed to be."

Bryan shared with his pastor, and later others, about this sense of something missing. They assured him he was fine. Still, he couldn't shake the belief there was more God was after.

Then God led Bryan to the Battle for the Heart retreat where he discovered "the whole rest of my heart."

As Bryan began to understand more of his heart and God's heart, he realized that a deceptive desire for success was sabotaging some of his deepest desires and limiting his capacity to love well.

What made success a deceptive desire? As mentioned earlier, deceptive desires are surface desires we pursue thinking they will fully satisfy deep desires. Under Bryan's drive for success were deeper desires. For love. For respect. To hear "Well done."

In childhood Bryan found those desires partly satisfied when he received positive affirmation for achievement. The grandfather he adored spent significant time with him, drilling him on schoolwork with flash cards and paying him for As. But he also witnessed his grandfather painfully reject someone close to him when that person failed. The stark contrast between the two experiences communicated to Bryan that if he performed well, he would be loved and that if he failed, he would be rejected.

Bryan developed a visceral belief that all love, including God's, was conditional. So, he pursued success in order to experience love and respect. He built a successful career, had an outwardly successful marriage, well-behaved children, and a respected role in church. He thought these things would give him what he most longed for. But someone who operates from a false belief that love is conditional is only able to offer conditional love in response. Consequently, Bryan's leadership style and the way he engaged with others in all areas of life, including his family, created distance and damage.

With his wife

"On the altar of achievement, perfection, and success, I sacrificed Christy's heart . . . My own lack of vulnerability only offered her a cold, hard, aloof, and arrogant man, a man hiding from his own failings and doing it all under the veneer of spiritual leadership."

With his children

"Even when I tried to love my children, I only offered performance-driven expectations."

With his coworkers

"My natural tendency was to run over people in the drive for results."

As Bryan grew in awareness of these relational disconnections, he had a moment of insight after an exchange with one of his sons. He came to the "devastating and depressing realization" that he risked passing on to his kids the same beliefs and self-protective strategies he had held onto his entire life. Something had to change.

Gradually, Bryan began lowering his defenses and opening his heart more fully to God's love. He began offering his vulnerable heart to others, asking for forgiveness where needed, and acknowledging his desires for respect, love, peace, and rest. The fruit of that inner heart work has been an increasing understanding that he is loved regardless of performance.

> I see now God loves me for who I am, not just for what I do. God's "Well done" is not based on my being able to manage $5 billion or $50 billion of kingdom assets. He's more concerned with how I'm engaging with the people who are important to him and to me. My need for respect, my need to earn my way into a loving relationship, sabotaged my ability to love others.

As Bryan experienced the Father's love and validation, he found freedom to love others without demanding respect or results. This brought satisfaction and fulfillment through deeper connection with God and others.

Bryan's focus at work shifted from pushing others to deliver results to helping them develop personally and caring about them as individuals while trusting God with the results. This new focus required Bryan to change his more reserved and aloof leadership style. He became more attentive to his heart and the hearts of others. In the process, Bryan experienced God satisfying his deep desires in unexpected ways.

> When I surrender the results to God, I experience more peace and rest. By allowing myself to be vulnerable with others, I open the door to authentic, mutual relationships that meet my deep desires for love and connection, and in most cases, lead to a greater level of respect.
>
> Results are still important, don't get me wrong. This is something I continue to battle. But at least I'm surrendering some level of the results, and I'm able to experience more of God's peace and rest, knowing that I've loved people well.

What about you? What desires do you pursue in ways that sabotage your capacity to love well? As people created to desire, we are all guilty, at times, of looking to people and experiences to satisfy our desires, believing they will give us what we most long for. We fail to realize the subtle ways Evil tempts us to choose pride and independence from God.

Evil Tempts Us to Choose the Way of Pride

In the Way of Pride, we seek to meet our own desires by choosing:

- **Independence:** I will do what I want to do when I want to do it.
- **Image Management:** I will project the image of who I want to be or who I think others want me to be.
- **Indulgence:** I will use my gifts and talents or self-medicate to meet my desires or avoid the pain of unmet desires.
- **Self-Inflation:** I will elevate myself using my talents, possessions, or people.

In Bryan's story, he discovered that independence and image management were the two primary ways he operated out of pride:

- **Independence:** He chose control and self-sufficiency as the way to meet his own needs and desires and his family's needs.
- **Image Management:** He sought to look the part of someone who had it all together as a solid, responsible leader afraid of nothing, who never failed.

Deceived by Evil, Bryan believed that being successful in business and other areas of life could satisfy his deep desire to hear "Well done" from his heavenly Father. What Bryan finally discovered is that his heavenly Father longed most of all for him to surrender his whole, authentic, vulnerable heart to divine love and to experience his Father's delight in him as his beloved son. Out of an increasingly secure identity, Bryan imperfectly but faithfully moved into his purpose to love God and others, including his team and the people God brought him to serve by managing their investments. As he grew in loving well, he increasingly heard the Father's "Well done."

Desires That Draw Us Away from God

As demonstrated in Bryan's story, sometimes even good desires draw us away from God.

Paul describes deceptive desires as evil because they flow out of the hardened or darkened places of our hearts (see Ephesians 4:17-22). These desires keep us trapped in our old way of life and unable to experience the fulfillment that comes with receiving God's love and acting on his purpose for us. Since these desires are evil, many people respond by trying to repress them. But this never works because God created us to desire.

Freedom comes not with repressing our desires but with opening our whole hearts to the light of God's love that reveals Evil's deception. In repentance, we allow God to break open the hardened places of our heart, to blow up the dams that block the flow of his love. With our hearts no longer darkened, we are then able to follow our deepest desires to the One who created us to experience those desires in union with him.

As Bryan connected more fully to his own heart and to God, he recognized and repented of the ways he operated from the Way of Pride by pursuing deceptive desires. As he chose the Way of Humility, he experienced God's love, grace, and truth changing his heart. He was increasingly able to rest in knowing he was loved. This freed him to live from his true identity and purpose as one who is loved and created to love. His underlying deep desires have not changed. But he now seeks to meet those desires in ways that move him toward greater connection with God and others. The chart below reflects these shifts in his beliefs and actions.

As you review the chart, note what stands out to you about Bryan's change and how it matches or differs from your own spiritual journey.

Figure 8.0

Bryan's Deep Desires	Living in the Way of Pride	Living in the Way of Humility
Respect	Believed respect was earned primarily through accomplishment, so he valued success over relationships.	Respect is based on "who I am" rather than "what I do." Accomplishment can still be a factor, but respect primarily comes from being the person he is created to be.

"Well done"	Equated "well done" with quantitative results.	Can hear "well done" from his Heavenly Father when he loves well, even if/when he doesn't succeed by the world's standard.
To love and be loved	Believed viscerally that love was conditional, contingent on performance; by valuing achievement over people, he sabotaged his desire for love and connection.	Can hear "well done" from his Heavenly Father when he loves well, even if/when he doesn't succeed by the world's standard.
Peace and rest	Unaware of this desire because life was consumed by "doing".	As he lives with a deeper sense of his identity and purpose, he is increasingly trusting God with the results. Trust gives him the peace and rest he longs for.

How Evil Tempts Us to Meet Our Desires Apart from God

God has designed us in such a way that our deepest desires—which act as a navigational system that points us to him—can only be fully satisfied in him.

Dr. Curt Thompson in his book *The Soul of Desire* says,

> That we seem to have a fathomless depth of wanting suggests that our longing, indeed, will be fulfilled only in a relationship of comparable infinite depth.[12]

The desires God has placed in us—the longings for peace, for joy, for security, for love—are so deep that only One of even greater depth can satisfy them. Saint Augustine of Hippo in his book *Confessions* states it this way:

> You have made us for yourself, and our hearts are restless until they rest in you (modern paraphrase).[13]

Our desires are all part of God's pursuit of us. He gives us desires that draw us to him, and we respond to his pursuit when we live in vulnerable dependence on him, trusting him to satisfy those desires, now in part and fully in eternity.

Evil seeks to disrupt intimacy, to draw us away from God by weakening or destroying our trust in him throughout our lives. This means that even though we may have a biblical understanding of trust, in moments of pressure—when our trust is being challenged—we don't fully believe God will meet our desires. When this happens, we look to ourselves and other people and experiences to answer our deepest heart questions.

Figure 8.1

Evil's Plan

Destroy trust, the valve that opens our hearts to God's love.

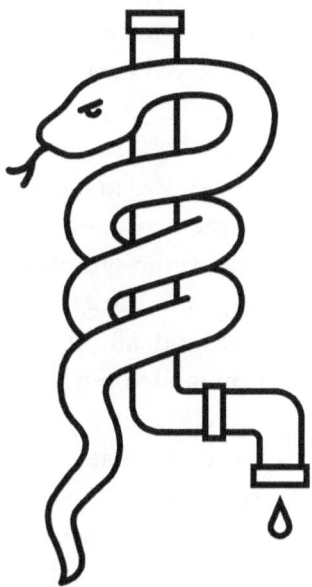

Am I Loved?

Why does Evil specifically attack our trust in God? Trust is like the valve that opens or closes our hearts to receive God's love. If, out of fear, we do not trust that his heart toward us is good, the valve stays closed. We stay cut off from intimate connection with

God, darkened in our understanding of our hearts. We may still function, but everything that flows from our shut-down hearts will be tainted in some measure by the deceitful desires that flourish most in the absence of God's love and light. Lacking trust in God to meet our deepest desires, we will seek to meet them independently in ways that violate who we are created to be as God's image bearers.

A sobering example of this is what happened in the Garden of Eden. There, even though Adam and Eve had only ever experienced God as trustworthy, Evil took an experience of ultimate beauty and glory and twisted it in such a way that Eve was deceived into doubting God's love.

"Did God really say . . . ?" (Genesis 3:1).

Imagine what the scene must have been like when Evil first posed that question. The fragrance of ripening fruit; the gentle warmth of sun-kissed skin; the lushness of grass underfoot; the symphony of sounds. And all around was provision rising from the ground, flourishing on trees. There was an abundance of food, all theirs to enjoy—except one. One tree that they were commanded not to eat from.

When Eve looked at the fruit of that tree, she saw that it "was good for food and pleasing to the eye, and also desirable for gaining wisdom" (v. 6). She trusted the serpent and herself to meet her desires for goodness, for beauty, and for wisdom to know what was good and what was evil.

How did Eve answer the question "Am I loved?" She did not believe God's love was enough that she could trust him with her deepest desires. Out of fear, she chose to meet her own desires. The valve allowing God's love to flow to Eve began to close, disrupting the intimate connection she once had with the Father.

Who am I?

Out of fear, Eve chose a new identity as an independent woman who decided for herself what was good and evil.

Why am I here?

She acted from a visceral belief that it was up to her to satisfy her own desires in her own way. She then invited Adam to join her. Together they fell from the glory of knowing God's love and revealing his love to one another and the world.

Evil does the same to us today. We all face the same choice: Will we choose independence, disrupted intimacy, and a life based on a distorted sense of our identity and purpose? Or will we choose, as Bryan ultimately did, to humbly trust God that we can be image bearers who reveal his glory?

But what about when the path to becoming who you're created to be, the path to revealing God's glory, requires embracing pain? This was the choice Abby faced in our next story. Would she let go of a deceptive desire to avoid pain, which she thought would lead to the experience of safety and peace, and choose the Way of Humility? In her courageous "yes," God has used her to rewrite the stories of three young girls.

From Fear and Independence to Trust and Vulnerable Dependence

Abby was twenty-eight when she joined our staff in 2010. A naturally empathic person, as a child, she developed a self-protective strategy of shutting down to avoid the overwhelming emotions she was too young to process. This gave her a sense of safety and control.

Shortly after coming on staff, she attended a Battle for the Heart retreat. While there, God began to show her the cost of her self-protective strategies. Here's Abby's story in her own words:

The Lord began to gently reveal that my deeply rooted fear of pain kept me from being the woman he had created me to be, someone who loved others in a way that allowed them to experience his heart. As God exposed my fear, he reminded me of a situation from a few years prior. My brother entered a season of pain greater than I could wrap my head around. My love for him was so deep that I could physically feel the pain he was going through.

This experience brought me face-to-face with my fears about God. I doubted his goodness in my brother's situation and struggled to believe anything redemptive could come of it.

As I saw my brother's pain and disillusionment, out of my desire for safety, I shut down my heart. I couldn't handle the depth of his pain or face my doubts about God. I struggled to reconcile a good God with such pain and suffering. I wondered if it was even possible to walk through life-altering pain and still believe God was good.

Despite my deep love for my brother, I chose to run away emotionally. In his hour of greatest need, I could not be present or engaged. Too overwhelmed by his pain, I avoided thinking about it, wishing it away almost like a child who thinks that by closing her eyes she can disappear. I even convinced myself that hiding was an act of faith, believing God didn't need me to reach my brother.

But God showed me, during the retreat, that my fears, not my faith, silenced me. My close relationship with my brother gave me a voice in his life no one else had. His painful trial was an opportunity to reveal God to him in a unique way, yet in the moment of pressure, I couldn't handle the heat.

When God brought this season to mind, I could see the painful cost of my selfish choice. For the first time, I glimpsed what was at stake beyond my own sense of safety. I was brokenhearted over what my shutting down must have communicated to him. I had a chance to reveal God's love, and I failed.

Abby's deceptive desire was to avoid pain to satisfy her deep desire for safety. Out of self-protection, she shut down her heart and emotionally withdrew, sabotaging her deep desire to love her brother.

As she faced the cost of satisfying her deep desire for safety by her own means, she had a choice to make: Would she continue in the Way of Pride, independently protecting her own heart, or would she embrace the Way of Humility, trusting God could help her through her pain and fears? Choosing humility, Abby repented and grieved that her failure to live out her true identity and purpose when her brother needed her had cost him greatly.

> In that place of gut-wrenching repentance and mourning, I realized that to be the woman God created me to be, I would have to enter pain and believe God would be present in it with me. I chose to believe with my whole heart that what I would find on the other side of this journey would be worth fighting for.

As Abby began opening the shut-down places of her heart to God and received his comfort, she gained courage to open her heart to others in pain. This required violating her protective strategies.

After the retreat, God continued to speak to Abby through prayer and scripture about surrender, trust, and love.

> Through God's pursuit I saw that it is only in surrendering control that I could find true rest and experience safety—two of my deep desires. As I engaged scripture, particularly 1 John 4:18 on perfect love casting out fear, I began to more clearly see my fear was greater than my understanding of God's love. I knew there had to be a shift. I needed to know God's love more deeply.
>
> It took two years before I felt some level of freedom from my fear of pain. I took baby steps while positioning myself and asking God: "Show me your heart toward me." I engaged with scripture and spent time meeting the Lord in worship and prayer. He was incredibly gentle and patient, responding at each step.

> And as I grew in trusting his heart toward me, I experienced increasing freedom to move into who he created me to be in his Larger Story. This included choosing to live from a heart open to the pain of others.

As Abby began connecting with God's heart in new ways, she was drawn to his heart for orphans.

> I had spent my life to that point determined I would never be a mother—the potential for pain was too risky. Yet God, in his goodness, would not allow me to live in a smaller, seemingly controlled story.
>
> Suddenly—surprisingly—I began to long to help children I didn't know come to understand that they are worth loving and protecting. My heart shattered when I considered children in homes that were not safe, where they questioned if they were loved or were worth fighting for. I wanted to be a channel of God's love to these children from hard places.
>
> In 2014, I drew every ounce of courage in my being and, with my husband, responded to God's leading to open our home and hearts to children in need. Over the next two years we walked through the ups and downs of fostering. The experience ultimately led to us adopting three precious sisters whose lives are marked by trauma.

Abby went from being someone whose fear kept her from being present with others in pain to a mother of three daughters whose lives were defined by pain. To be the mother she longs to be, the mother her girls need, she has to consistently embrace pain. Many days she calls and shares that pain, and all I can do is sit with her in the pain, pray for her, and trust with her that God's heart toward her and her girls is good, and he will, in his time and way, bring forth resurrection, life, and glory for her and for them.

We see in Abby's story that Evil often hunts us through our desires in areas related to our greatest strengths and purpose. In Abby's case, Evil hunted her through her deep desires for *safety, security, and protection*. To meet those desires, Abby turned inward, shutting down parts of her heart and choosing a form of control that gave an illusion of safety. But as she opened her heart to her Father's pursuit, she experienced the intimacy of his love, grace, and truth which drew her to himself and revealed her deceptions. As she responded with repentance, God drew her into a deeper knowing of his love, increasing her trust in the goodness of God's heart toward her. This empowered her to embrace her true identity, the unique person shaped out of the pain of her life, and to fulfill her purpose of revealing God's heart by offering three girls the chance to experience *safety, security, and protection* through adoption.

In both Abby's and Bryan's story we see them choose to move away from the deceptive desires of the Way of Pride. They instead choose the Way of Humility, surrender their desires to God, and trust him to satisfy those desires in his time and way. As Abby and Bryan continue to choose humility, God increases both their capacity to love well and the impact of their love.

Where do you find yourself on that journey? Where do you still battle with fear and trust?

We look to Jesus and see the ultimate battle between fear and trust. Jesus chose to trust his Father's heart all the way to the cross for the joy of reconnecting our hearts to God's heart and restoring us to the glory and honor he created us for.

FOR DEEPER CONNECTION

Personalize

Tell of a time you pursued a surface desire only to find the pleasure you thought it would bring fell short. (See the Desires chart in the Toolbox for help with these questions.)

Gain Awareness

As you think about that experience, what are you feeling?

What deep desire(s) do you think that surface desire connects to? To answer, it may be helpful to first identify the deep desires that are most significant to you.

Respond

Father, I confess that I sometimes struggle to believe your heart is truly good. I fear I'll always live with the pain of unmet desires. Help me turn to you and experience your perfect love casting out my fear. I thank you that I can also turn to you with my doubts and questions and receive comfort and insight. I ask you to set my heart to truly know you, to love you, and to be loved by you.

Part 3

The Way of Humility

The path to deepening connection with your own heart, God, and others

CHAPTER 9

Is There Another Way?

How the Father prepares his son for the cross

Larry

In past chapters we've journeyed from the beautiful, flourishing fullness of life and love that is Eden to the harsh, desolate reality of the fall with lives distorted by fear and pride.

We've explored a way back to fullness, becoming wholehearted, as we increasingly connect to our hearts, God's heart, and the hearts of others. Through these connections, we experience divine intimacy, identity, and purpose. Through stories, we've discovered that to experience this fullness, we must let go of the Way of Pride energized by fear and control and choose the Way of Humility, energized by love and trust. Yet it can be difficult to let go of what we know for the insecurity of the unknown; to believe the words of our heavenly Father when our earthly experience screams the opposite.

This requires faith that is "confidence in what we hope for and assurance about what we do not see" (Hebrews 11:1). So how do we gain confidence in the God who promises to never leave or forsake us, in the God who promises to protect us when we experience the disappointment of unfulfilled dreams, abandonment, betrayal, or violation? How do we come to hope and trust in this God we cannot see?

We look to the story of Jesus—a story so familiar to many of us that we often fail to truly see the God who chose to become fully human so that he might become "the pioneer and perfecter of faith" (Hebrews 12:2).

While we seek to honor that the incarnate Jesus is both fully divine and fully human (see Philippians 2:6–8), we want to stretch our hearts to see into the heart of a Father preparing his Son for the trials he would face, and the heart of a Son responding to his Father in faith. In the Way of Humility, Jesus:

- surrendered to the love of his Father;
- opened his authentic, vulnerable heart to love, in community;
- embraced God in suffering; trusted his goodness; and
- trusted his Father's promise to bring forth resurrection, life, and glory in his time and way.

In the coming chapters we will apply the story of Jesus to our own lives as he invites us, by faith in him as our pioneer, into the Way of Humility. Our starting point is in two gardens—one where faith was abandoned, and one where it was perfected.

A Tale of Two Gardens

On the night of his arrest, under the cover of darkness, Jesus led his disciples from the intimacy of the Passover meal to a familiar place on the Mount of Olives. Lacking the lushness of Eden, the Garden of Gethsemane was a place where olive trees flourished amid the arid, dry climate—a place where olives were crushed to bring forth oil.

Painfully aware of the coming crushing of his own life, Jesus invited his three closest disciples to watch and pray as he connected to the heart of his Father. As he entered a gut-wrenching struggle—an anguish so deep he sweated drops of blood—he cried out, "*Abba*, Father . . . everything is possible for you. Take this cup from me" (Mark 14:36).

Three times he asked. Three times he heard the Father's no. Yet, in faith he trusted his Father's goodness behind the no.

Eve, in a *flourishing* garden, chose not to trust the Father's heart.

She and Adam ate of the forbidden tree, plunging mankind into darkness. Jesus, in a *barren* garden, chose to trust his Father's heart, to willingly give himself up to death on a tree that he might overcome darkness to become "the light of all mankind" (John 1:4).

Two strikingly different gardens. Two strikingly different outcomes. So how did Jesus succeed where Adam, Eve, and every other human being have failed?

The easy answer would be to dismiss Christ's humanity and credit his obedience to his divine nature. But Jesus was "made like [us], fully human in every way" (Hebrews 2:17).

Jesus' incarnation as an infant indicates that God's plan for Jesus, as for us, involved a maturation process. As the eternal Son, Jesus clearly knew the Larger Story, but as a human son, he had to discover and embrace his part in that story.

What was at stake? The eternal desire of the Father, Son, and Spirit to enter into a mutual, loving relationship with human beings—the bride of Christ—through which his divine glory overflows from our hearts, filling the universe and satisfying our deepest desires in ways we can now only taste.

So, let's pull back the curtains into eternity to glimpse how the Father prepares his Son for his part in the Story.

The Father Prepared Jesus Through His Family and Community

After the Father had chosen the woman who would be the mother of his incarnate Son, he sent an angel to share with Mary that she had "found favor with God" (Luke 1:30). The angel then shared the stunning, life-changing news that she would conceive a child who would be the Messiah!

At first, Mary was fearful and wondered how this could be since she was a virgin. Yet she responded in humility and faith: "I am the Lord's servant. . . . May your word to me be fulfilled" (v. 38).

After Jesus was born, an angel appeared to Joseph in a dream to warn him of Herod's plans to find and kill Jesus. The angel instructed Joseph to take Mary and Jesus to seek refuge in Egypt. Eventually, angels appeared again to tell Joseph it was safe for the family to return to Israel and eventually Nazareth.

What must it have been like for Jesus growing up to hear his mother and father share stories of their faith, of his birth, and of the awe-inspiring angels? Surely they shared how they came to be refugees in Egypt and how, in each situation, they trusted in God's divine, orchestrating love and goodness.

As a young boy, Jesus trained in the Jewish synagogue to become a man responsible to God, to the scriptures, and to the community. At age twelve, he traveled with his parents to Jerusalem for Passover, engaging with the teachers of the law in the temple. But as his parents began their return home, they discovered Jesus was not with them! Returning to Jerusalem, they eventually found him in the temple. Mary, out of a mother's distress, rebuked him.

Jesus' response seems to indicate surprise that his mother doesn't see what he sees. "Why were you looking for me? . . . Didn't you know I had to be in my Father's house?" (Luke 2:49).

Jesus' reference to the temple as his "Father's house" speaks of a boy intimately acquainted with his heavenly Father—a boy who so believed in his identity that he could boldly say, "This temple is my Father's house." That's audacious!

An alternate reading of this verse is "that I must be about my Father's business" (KJV). What was the Father's business? To reconnect human beings to divine love so they would overflow with love, filling the earth with his glory.

Yet his time to begin his ministry had not yet come, so Jesus returned home. There he continued to grow in "wisdom and stature, and in favor with God and man" (Luke 2:52). Surely Jesus grew in his intimate knowing of his Father's love and in his understanding of his identity and divine purpose. I wonder when he fully grasped this purpose would mean a sacrificial death on a cross. Perhaps it was when he read about the Suffering Servant who would be "crushed" as he bore our pain, shame, and sin (Isaiah 53:5-6, 10) that he heard the Father whisper, "This is who you are. This is the family business."

Regardless of how Jesus' story unfolded, from his experience in the temple the Father took approximately eighteen more years to carefully, lovingly prepare Jesus to fulfill his purpose of becoming the fully human pioneer and perfecter of faith.

Surrender to Divine Love and Validation

When the time came, how would the Father prepare his son before launching the greatest rescue mission in human history? What did he most want his Son to know?

There was no elaborate commissioning fit for a coming King. There were no strategy sessions or final tips on how to succeed. There was simply a loving Father orchestrating a divine experience of intimate connection with his Son. As you read Mark's description, notice the Father's focus:

> At that time Jesus came from Nazareth in Galilee and was baptized by John in the Jordan. Just as Jesus was coming up out of the water, he saw heaven being torn open and the Spirit descending on him like a dove. And a voice came from heaven: "You are my Son, whom I love; with you I am well pleased." (Mark 1:9–11)

As the Holy Spirit descends upon Jesus, he hears the Father's voice speaking to the deepest desires and questions of his human heart.

Am I loved?

The Father communicates his intimate love as he tenderly calls Jesus "my Son, whom I love."

Who am I?

He is the Son who is so loved, *his very identity* is in simply *being* the Son who is loved. To the Father, those terms are inseparable! In the ESV, "My Son, whom I love" has an alternate reading. In the experience of being loved, the verb becomes a noun: "My Son, the Beloved."

Then the Father's love bursts into "pleasure," "pride" (MSG), and "delight" (TLB).

Why am I here?

In the Spirit's descent and the Father's expression of delight, we see a glimpse of Jesus' purpose from Isaiah 42:1. There the Father speaks of the servant he has "chosen, in whom he delights, the one he puts his Spirit on . . . to bring justice to the nations."[14]

The overall focus of this scene is the Father's overwhelming love for Jesus and his validation of his Son's identity. His purpose is present, but it is in the background.

Why does God focus more on love and identity? Even though we cannot fully know, as a father myself, I believe that the Father's heart so overflows with love, joy, and pride that he tears open the heavens, sends his Spirit, and passionately shares with his beloved son!

I wonder what the fully human Son experienced as the Father directly spoke to the deepest questions and desires of his heart. I wonder if the Father's beaming face was like sunshine poured into his being, flooding him with love and a deep sense of his identity. As he heard the Father's voice, as he experienced the presence of the Spirit, did all the years of preparation—of waiting, of reverent surrender, and of obedience—feel worth it? Did he experience an ever-deepening conviction to fulfill his divine purpose?

Regardless of what Jesus may have experienced, the Father knew that the most critical element in the divine rescue mission was trust.

This intimate expression of love, identity, and purpose concludes a thirty-year preparation process of building trust between a Divine Father and a human Son. Then, out of his love, the Father sent his Son to the wilderness where this trust would be severely tested and ultimately strengthened.

Embracing God in Suffering— Trusting His Goodness

Luke tells us that "Jesus, full of the Holy Spirit, left the Jordan and was led by the Spirit into the wilderness, where for forty days he was tempted by the devil. He ate nothing during those days, and at the end of them he was hungry" (v. 4:1–2). The word *tempted* can mean either tempted or tested. Satan tempted Jesus to doubt and disobey—just as he did with Eve.

For forty days and nights Jesus fasted and prayed, severely depleting his body and strength. It is then that Evil attempted to disrupt the intimate connection between Father and Son. As New Testament scholar R. T. France states,

> The focus of the testing agenda is indicated by the clause which introduces the devil's first two suggestions, "If you are the son of God." The special relationship with God which has just been authoritatively declared in the Jordan is now under scrutiny ... The devil is trying to drive a wedge between the newly declared son and his father.[15]

The implied meaning of Evil's words? If you are the Son of God, you don't have to keep waiting, wondering when your Father will come through. You can make it happen. You can turn these stones into bread. You don't have to choose the path of suffering any longer.

In a display of vulnerable dependence and trust in his Father's goodness, Jesus responds with scripture: "It is written: 'Man shall not live on bread alone, but on every word that comes from the mouth of God'" (Matthew 4:4).

What words had he been hanging onto for forty days? The words memorized in his childhood, the Father's spoken words of love and identity, and the wholehearted experience of the Father's delight and pride in him. They fed him; they sustained him through pain and suffering. His faith in the God of those words solidified his trust and protected him from the Evil one.

Twice more, Evil sought to drive a wedge between Father and Son, tempting the Son to doubt that his Father would come through; to wonder if there was another way to the glory set before him—one that did not involve suffering. But in each attack, Jesus' trust in the Father's love and his own identity and purpose held. That trust would be increasingly tested in the suffering yet to come. But why did it have to be this way?

The writer of Hebrews explains:

> During the days of Jesus' life on earth, he offered up prayers and petitions with fervent cries and tears to the one who could save him from death, and he was heard because of his reverent submission. Son though he was, he learned obedience from what he suffered and, once made perfect, he became the source of eternal salvation for all who obey him. (Hebrews 5:7–9)

Why did the sinless Son have to "learn" obedience?

As with faith, obedience is perfected as we practice it. It is through Jesus' experience of testing that his faith, trust, and obedience are proven. As one commentary explains:

> Though he was the eternal Son of God, it was necessary for him as the incarnate Son to learn obedience—not that he was ever disobedient, but that he was called on to obey to an extent he had never before experienced. The temptations he faced were real and the battle for victory was difficult, but where Adam failed and fell, Jesus resisted and prevailed. His humanity was thereby completed, "made perfect" and on the basis of this perfection he could become "the source of eternal salvation".[16]

Pause and consider the implications of this.

How many times have you, like me, been tempted to doubt God's goodness in suffering?

How many times have you struggled to trust and obey?

Looking back on my own life, through many trials and suffering, I see lots of struggles and some failures. Yet I see how God, in his gracious kindness, used my struggling, imperfect faith in the pioneer and perfecter of faith to take me deeper into his love and purposes.

Ongoing Surrender to the Father's Love and Validation

As the excruciating suffering of Gethsemane and the cross drew near, the Father knew Jesus would have to trust to a degree he never had before. So, the Father prepared him through another intimate experience of divine love that would propel him into his eternal purpose.

As you read, try to imagine a spectacular light show with biblical stars!

Jesus took Peter, James, and John up a mountain to pray with him. As they arrived, Jesus was transfigured before their very eyes: "His face shone like the sun, and his clothes became as white as the light" (Matthew 17:1–2).

For just a moment the three disciples saw "his true nature . . . glorious and majestic . . . that will be revealed to all the world at the time of his return."[17] For a moment Jesus actually experienced the glory coming after the cross—the glory he had with the Father and will have through all eternity.

In the midst of his shining glory, the Father sent Moses and Elijah, who symbolize the coming of the Messianic Age now being fulfilled in Jesus.[18] They spoke to Jesus about his coming departure, his rescue mission freeing those "enslaved by their fear of death," into the "freedom and glory of the children of God" (Hebrews 2:14–15; Romans 8:21).

Then the Father returned to the focus of intimacy and identity.

As Peter described the scene, Jesus "received honor and glory from God the Father when the voice came to him from the Majestic Glory, saying, 'This is my Son, whom I love; with him I am well pleased'" (2 Peter 1:17–18).

What is his glory and honor? His glory is in his identity as the beloved Son. His honor is to fulfill his purpose, to give his life to bring many sons and daughters back to the glory God created us for. How? Jesus becomes the pioneer for us. He blazes the path for us. To do that, God had to make him "perfect through what he suffered" (Hebrews 2:10).

Jesus is now ready for the next step in his path: the agony of Gethsemane, the arid place where olives are crushed. For thirty-three years the Father has been preparing for this moment, the ultimate test of trust between a Father and his Son.

As human beings created in the image of a loving God, we do not desire to experience extreme suffering, but from before the creation of the world, the eternal Son planned this path, desired this path, and chose this path. Now as the fully human Son, he has to live it out in his fully human experience.

As he enters the most intense suffering of his life, what might be happening in Jesus' whole heart? We can never fully know the depths of what he experienced as he now faced the cost of what he chose in eternity. Yet whatever it was, we do know it involved trust because Jesus is the "pioneer and perfecter of faith" (Hebrews 12:2).

As you read what Jesus experienced at Gethsemane, seek to pause and let your whole heart be affected by what you see in the heart of Jesus.

Trusting God for Resurrection, Life, and Glory

What Was Jesus Thinking?

Aware of the intense battle coming, Jesus asks Peter, James, and John—those closest to him—to be with him, to watch and pray for him.

Jesus knew his part in the Story. Now slowly read what Jesus knew before the world was created, what he came to understand about his purpose when he was a fully human boy, and what he now faced as he experienced suffering at a depth he had never felt before:

> Surely he took up our pain and bore our suffering, yet we considered him punished by God, stricken by him, and afflicted. But he was pierced for our transgressions, he was crushed for our iniquities; the punishment that brought us peace was on him, and by his wounds we are healed. We all, like sheep, have gone astray, each of us has turned to our own way; and the LORD has laid on him the iniquity of us all. (Isaiah 53:4–6)

What Was He Feeling?

Out of the fullness of this knowing, Jesus began to be deeply distressed and troubled to the point he shared with his brothers, "My soul is overwhelmed with sorrow to the point of death. . . . Stay here and keep watch" (Mark 14:34).

The words used here reveal Jesus feeling a "deep inner revulsion at what was coming . . . a shuddering horror as he faces the dreadful prospect before him."[19] This took him into an anguish so deep, prayers so fervent, that "his sweat was like drops of blood falling to the ground" (Luke 22:44).

This is far beyond the anguish of facing the physical suffering of the cross. This is the Suffering Servant taking into himself the pain and suffering of the whole world and the punishment for the rebellion, distortions, and sin of the whole world. Because of all this, he would bear the unfathomable pain of, in some way, being disconnected, "forsaken" by his Father (Matthew 27:46).

What Did He Desire?

In the depth of those overwhelming feelings, he desired another way, a way that did not require him to drink this shuddering cup of horror. He *really* desired another way! So, he cried out to the Father three times. In the midst of his agonizing cries I wonder if he remembered his

Father's proud voice at the baptism; remembered how he trusted the Father's promises in the agony of the wilderness; and remembered the glory of the transfiguration.

I wonder if, at this point, Jesus anticipated the joy of revealing the glory of the Trinity upon his resurrection; the joy of destroying the works of the devil; the joy of bridging the gap between fallen human beings and divine love through his sacrificial death; the joy of returning to the heavenly glory he had known and sitting at the right hand of the Father; and the joy of again hearing those precious words "This is my Son, whom I love; with him I am well pleased" (Matthew 3:17).

As Jesus faced the cross and saw "the joy set before him" (Hebrews 12:2), how did the fully human Jesus respond?

What Did He Choose?

In the greatest suffering of human history, Jesus connected to his Father's love for him, his love for the Father, and his love for you. In that love he chose to trust his Father's goodness. He chose to trust his Father's promise to bring him through death and hell and into resurrection, life, and glory.

In the full light of the next day, Roman soldiers nailed the Suffering Servant to a tree, fulfilling the prophecies of Isaiah 52 and 53. Jesus "who knew no sin" became sin for us (2 Corinthians 5:21). When he took his last breath, he cried out, "It is finished" (John 19:30). Through it all, Jesus trusted the goodness of his Father.

Just like the Father prepared the Son, he longs to prepare you to fulfill your part in his Story. Jesus opened the Way as he "humbled himself by becoming obedient to death—even death on a cross!" (Philippians 2:8). What will you choose?

Will you humble yourself by choosing the Way of Humility that you might become the person the Father created you to be and that Jesus endured the cross that you might become?

Will you

- surrender to divine love;
- open your whole heart to love in community;
- embrace God in suffering while trusting his goodness; and
- trust God's promises to bring resurrection, life, and glory in his time and his way?

In the remaining chapters, we will see how, as we surrender to divine love through union with Christ, the pioneer and perfecter of our faith, there is

> Nothing between us and God, our faces shining with the brightness of his face. And so we are transfigured much like the Messiah, our lives gradually becoming brighter and more beautiful as God enters our lives and we become like him. (2 Corinthians 3:18 MSG)

FOR DEEPER CONNECTION

Personalize

Jesus learned trust through suffering. How does that match your own experience of suffering?

Gain Awareness

What happens in you as you consider that just as you experience suffering, the fully human Jesus also experienced suffering?

As you reflect on the current painful places in your journey, what do you most long for from the Father right now?

Respond

As you feel led, share honestly with the Father about your pain, about your desire for another way. Open your heart to the comfort of the Father who loves you with the same love he has for his Son and speaks to you: You are my child, whom I love; with you I am well pleased.

CHAPTER 10

Tell Me I'm a Good Man

Moving from "earn this" to "receive this"

Larry

In the award-winning movie *Saving Private Ryan*, six men set out to rescue Private James Ryan, the fourth and only surviving son of a bereaved mother. The leader of the rescue mission, Captain John Miller is mortally wounded in a battle while on the mission.

At the end of his life James visits the Normandy memorial to honor the man who saved his life. With his family behind him and his wife beside him, he looks at the stone grave marker.

Poignant memories flash before him. He's watching Captain Miller dying on the bridge where he was shot. As Miller looks into James's eyes, he tries to speak to him. With his last bit of strength, Miller pulls himself up, and James leans in to hear the captain whisper with his final breath, "James, earn this. Earn it."[20]

Decades later, James returns to the grave, kneels in front of the marker, and finally says to Captain Miller, "Every day I think about what you said to me that day on the bridge. I've tried to live my life the best that I could. I hope that was enough. I hope that at least in your eyes, I've earned what you all have done for me."[21]

James then turns to his wife with longing in his eyes: "Tell me I am a good man. Tell me I've led a good life." She looks at the grave marker and back at him, clearly aware of the question that has haunted them for decades. With compassion and love she responds, "Yes, you are."[22]

That day on the bridge, in the intimacy of life and death, Captain Miller—an older man, a revered leader, possibly a father figure—spoke into the deepest questions of James' heart.

Captain Miller's words placed an almost unbearable weight upon a young man longing to prove himself worthy of Miller's sacrifice. And don't we all feel that weight at times? Don't we all have questions that subconsciously drive us to succeed, to prove our value, to show ourselves worthy of love and respect?

James turns to the memory of Captain Miller, then to the intimacy of his relationship with his wife. Yet regardless of how much she loved him or how many times she told him yes, it was never enough because deep within, James had been stamped with an identify of "earn this."

That identity, that stamp, ultimately comes from the fall because, disconnected from God's unconditional love, we all believe, in some way, we must earn love, approval, sometimes even the gift of life itself.

Then in the heart of an impressionable young man, Miller reaffirms that stamp. For the rest of his life, James questions whether he earned Miller's sacrifice on his behalf. We hear his desperation for reassurance when he says to his wife, "Tell me I'm a good man. Tell me I've led a good life."

If we are honest with ourselves, we can identify with James in some way. This is the human condition. Even after we come to Christ, we keep going to people or experiences to validate us and to answer the questions that linger in the depth of our hearts.

The Only Authority That Can Validate You

So, what is validation? Validation authenticates the reality or essence of something. It comes from an authority with the right and capacity to verify that reality. For example, if I travel overseas, I need a United States passport. The US State Department is the only entity with authority to *validate* US citizenship. They stamp my passport with the official seal authenticating my identity as a US citizen and empowering me to fulfill my purpose of traveling overseas.

When I travel to a foreign country, the agent of that government who checks my passport looks carefully at the stamp. If all is in order, the agent stamps my passport to affirm my identity as a US citizen. Validation *makes* something officially acceptable or approved. Affirmation *recognizes* what the appropriate authority has already done.

The only one who can officially speak to your identity and purpose is the One who designed and created you! But he doesn't speak as an impersonal government agency. He speaks as your heavenly Father out of an intimate, joyful love, just as he spoke to his beloved Son.

When God validates us, he answers our questions about our value and worthiness to be loved. Then, people and experiences affirm what God has validated. But if we do not hear the Father's voice breaking through the armor created in our past, if his words of love do not permeate our hearts, we will continue to look to people and experiences for value and purpose. Their affirmation only lasts for a moment, and then we need more. We become like James who kept asking his wife to "Tell me I am a good man. Tell me I've led a good life!"

So, then, how does God reach the depth of our heart with words of validation? In the same way he did for Jesus.

In the last chapter, we dove into how the heavenly Father prepared his incarnate Son to fulfill his divine purpose. The Father focused on the most critical question to the success of the mission: will their relationship of love and trust hold in the most intense suffering in human history?

To ensure the strength of Jesus' trust in his love, the Father communicated consistently and in various ways his love for his Son, Jesus' identity as the beloved Son, and Jesus' calling to love sacrificially. The Father also tested their relationship and strengthened it. Jesus consistently responded in the Way of Humility. Together, they built a loving, trusting relationship that held all the way through the cross.

What the Father did for Jesus, he does for us. To prepare us to fulfill our divine purpose, he focuses on building a relationship of love and trust. The Father comes to us, pursuing us with his love. As we begin to trust his heart, we take the first step in the Way of Humility: we surrender to divine love. We open our whole hearts to receive the truth of God's love and validation in a way that satisfies our deepest desires, affects our feelings, captivates our thoughts, and energizes us to act out of our true identity.

As we grow in trust, we take another step: we open our hearts to God's love in community that affirms what God has validated.

When we respond, even imperfectly, to God's pursuit, he graciously builds a solid foundation of wholehearted trust. When the storms of suffering come, we may falter or fail, but our trust in God's goodness continues to grow so that one day, just like Jesus, we can say, "I have brought you glory on earth by finishing the work you gave me to do" (John 17:4).

How do we experience God's voice of love and validation? Through the Word, through direct revelation, and through four divine experiences: Creation, Redemption, Restoration, and Consummation.

Let's take a closer look.

God's Love and Validation at Creation

When God created human beings out of love, he intimately shaped Adam and Eve with his hands, breathed life into them, and then placed something of his own essence in them—he stamped them with his image. That stamp said, "You are mine." At the core of our being, our very identity is divine image bearers—his beloved sons and daughters—with the capacity to reveal and represent him.

As God looked upon Adam and Eve and all of his creation, he responded, "Very good." This goodness speaks to creation functioning in harmony with God's desire, God's purpose. That harmony brings the Creator great joy!

God's love and validation isn't something we earned, and it isn't something we can lose. It's a gift!

Evil Distorts Identity

But, as mentioned in chapter 8, Evil goes straight for Eve's trust in God's goodness. She fears God won't give her what she desires, so she chooses independence, inviting Adam to join her. It seems that in some way, Adam's desire to experience Eve's love and validation overwhelmed his desire for God's love and validation. So, he chose Eve. Now disconnected from God, Evil stamps them with the name "Distorted."

The beautiful gift of God's freely given love is distorted from "receive this" to "earn this."

Yet, thousands of years later David praises the God whose hands of love knit him together in his mother's womb, who created his innermost being. He is "fearfully and wonderfully made" (Psalm 139). David reminds us that in the intimacy of creation, God named human beings as beloved image bearers.

The good news is that the fall distorted our understanding of God's love for us and our identity in him, but God's divine stamp of love and validation remained unchanged.

God's Love and Validation Through Redemption

When God the Father, Son, and Holy Spirit chose to create human beings, they knew Adam and Eve would fall from glory into disconnection, distortion, and death. They knew that the Father would have to "crush" his beloved Son to redeem and restore us to the glory and honor he created us for (see Isaiah 53:10).

So the Father sent his Son. As Jesus hung dying on a cross, he cried out, "It is finished! (John 19:30). It is as if, with his last breath, he whispered to us, "Receive this," freeing us from the distorted "Earn this."

What does Jesus want us to receive? The free gift of forgiveness that opens the way for us to receive the free gift of his life. Jesus makes the Father known to us so that the very love the Father has for Jesus may be in us (see John 17:26). In this verse, Jesus twice uses the word *known*, a word that speaks of intimate, wholehearted knowing. In our knowing of the Father, we, in some mysterious way, experience the same love the Father has for Jesus. Pause and let that truth sink in!

Think back to chapter 9 when we contemplated the magnificent, joy-filled moment when the Father tore open the curtain of heaven and authoritatively, passionately declared, "This is my beloved Son, with whom I am well pleased" (Matthew 3:17 ESV).

Jesus prays that you will believe in the depths of your heart that as the Father sees you, he tears open the curtains of heaven and authoritatively, passionately declares: "You are my child, my beloved, in whom I am well pleased."

The Father's glorious face shines upon you with delight. He not only loves you, but he likes who he created you to be and who you are becoming in Christ. As you risk opening your heart to dare believe the radical depths of his love, your deepest desires become satisfied, your deepest questions answered.

Christ, the perfect image of the Father (see Hebrews 1:3) redeems the fallen, distorted image within us. We are new creations in Christ with the capacity to live in the fullness of the image of God—revealing his glory, his character, and acting on his behalf. This is a settled, eternal reality that becomes a lived experience as we increasingly respond to Christ through the Way of Humility.

God's Love and Validation Through Restoration

Jesus started life from a point of intimate connection with the Father. We start life from a place of disconnection. If Jesus needed to consistently hear the voice of his Father's love and validation, how much more do we?

This is the voice I heard in the devastation of Larry the Achiever in 2001 when, in desperation, I cried out to God and heard his voice validating me: "You are my son, whom I love, in whom I am well pleased."

This is the essence of the Christian life: to continually discover the unfathomable love and pleasure of our heavenly Father. As we do, he reveals places where the stamp of Evil runs deep and invites us to open our authentic, vulnerable hearts to go deep into his love, grace, and truth in community.

We don't have to earn the redemptive work of Christ, but we do have to respond to it—by surrendering to his love and cooperating with his ongoing work of restoration, becoming who we are and who we are meant to be: beloved daughters and sons, partners with the Trinity in revealing his glory on the earth.

From this place we have the security and confidence to step out and take risks in the kingdom.

Jesus illustrated taking risks for the kingdom in his parable of three servants and a master from Matthew 25:14-30. In the story, the master went on a journey. He called his servants and "entrusted his wealth to them" (v. 14). The master invited his servants into partnership with him as he lavishly gave "five bags of gold to one, to another two bags, and to another one bag, each according to his ability" (v. 15).

In this partnership, the master expected his partners to boldly take risks with what he had entrusted to them. Two servants did; one did not. What was the difference? Their view of the Master. The one who didn't risk believed that his master's heart was hard, so acting in fear, he hid his bag of gold.

Upon his return, the master said to each of the two who trusted and risked, "Well done, good and faithful servant. You have been faithful over a little; I will set you over much. Enter into the joy of your master" (v. 21, 23 ESV).

Note that what makes the master most joyful is not what they did but who they were: good and faithful servants. As we walk in the Way of Humility, surrendering to divine love, God validates our goodness.

Good servants fulfill God's design and desires for them to partner with him, to take risks with him, to reveal his glory through the assignments he gives them.

Faithful servants consistently step out in faith, believing God's heart is good toward them, even if they fail. And when they do fail, they receive his grace—not condemnation—as he picks them up and sends them out to risk again.

Many Christians struggle to hear their loving heavenly Father say, "Well done, good and faithful servant. Enter into my joy." Because of the distorted thought "Earn this," we struggle to believe that God could rejoice over us. Yet the truth is, God is joyful simply because we are good sons and daughters who are faithfully, imperfectly cooperating with him, our good Father, to reveal his glory.

As I've grown in entering into my heavenly Father's joyful delight, it is an exhilarating experience that increases my faith for the next assignment and inspires me to press on toward the eternal joy yet to come.

God's Love and Validation Through Consummation

In the book of Revelation, the apostle John sees a vision of the consummation of God's Larger Story as "a new heaven and a new earth" descend from heaven. He sees the Holy City prepared "as a bride beautifully dressed for her husband" shining "with the glory of God" (Revelation 21:1–2; 9–11).

The intimacy with us God desires and the intimacy with him we desire will be complete in the union of the bride and Christ. This consummation fulfills our identity: we are so loved that we are now Jesus' beloved bride. Likewise, our purpose is complete: we shine with God's glory and will reign with him forever in the eternal city.

In this striking image, all our desires are fulfilled, all our deepest questions answered as faith is perfected. As we see face to face, we fully know and are fully known in the eternal union of love (see 1 Corinthians 13:12; 1 John 3:2; Revelation 21:3–4). Through this union we play our unique part as fully restored human beings revealing and representing God in the new heaven and the new earth (see Genesis 1:26–28; Revelation 22:3–5). This is who we are; this is what we do for all eternity.

Until then we simply continue to respond in the Way of Humility as the Father lovingly speaks into our hearts preparing us for Consummation.

How Do We Hear the Validating Voice of the Father?

God speaks to us in many ways including ways we've focused on: Christ within us, the scriptures made alive by the Spirit, and the words of fellow believers in the body of Christ.

Often, as we open our hearts to hear the Father's validation, God gives us a new name that represents the changed person we are becoming. Our core identity is always a beloved image bearer. But these new names reveal something of the unique glory expressed through us, such as when God renamed Abram "Abraham," meaning "the father of many nations." In my case, God replaced my identity as Larry the Achiever with a new identity of Larry the Beloved. As you've seen, despite this new name, I still need to continually hear the truth of God's love for me, which happens as I choose the Way of Humility, starting with surrender to God's love. But as mentioned earlier, God also uses our brothers and sisters to help us hear God's voice of truth as they affirm or recognize what God has already validated. This vulnerable second step in the Way of Humility requires us to open our hearts to the love of God in community.

In multiple environments I've seen Christ speaking to a person through his body of believers revealing his face of love, compassion, comfort, and conviction. These experiences powerfully echo God's intimate, validating voice of identity and purpose and help blow up the dams of visceral beliefs, and free our hearts to be wellsprings of living water. This is heart-to-heart gospel transformation.

Here is one such story shared by Robby, one of our Battle for the Heart alumni.

At age twenty-eight, I experienced my first Battle for Men's Hearts retreat. In the following months, as I continued the work with my small team of men, I discovered how, from an early age, Evil named me "Incapable."

For the next few years, I kept coming back to retreats to serve as a team facilitator and eventually a speaker. At age thirty-six I stood in front of a room of men, mostly older than myself, with more educational and vocational success. Many of them I knew and deeply respected.

I shared my story of eight years of deepening surrender to God's love and repentance that opened my heart to viscerally believe that I am his beloved son. In that process God renamed me "Able." My time of sharing felt raw and vulnerable, yet I had a sense of personal pride in how I had delivered my story with passion, skill, and humility.

After I spoke, Larry and I met in his room with a small group of veteran leaders for a time of sharing, prayer, and affirmation. Larry invited me to pause and consider what God might be saying to me about me or about my sharing. Despite how satisfied I'd been moments earlier, I now experienced Evil's temptation to believe old lies. I hit a concrete wall of an old, deep belief that I am stupid and have nothing to offer.

Tears welled up in my eyes when I said, "I don't believe I belong in this room." Just minutes before, I had boldly declared that old identity of mine dead. Yet this block in my heart was tangible and seemed immovable.

After I shared, I saw fire in Larry's eyes. He was determined to see that concrete block crumble. Speaking to the depth of my heart, Larry spoke directly to my truest self, "You belong in this room."

His words collided with the lies and barely did anything. Tears ran down my face as Larry said again, "You belong in this room." Then he paused and said again, "You belong in this room."

Each time I could sense a chunk of unbelief being removed. In the uncomfortableness of the moment, I clamped my jaw and tried not to look away. I wanted this to end as soon as possible, yet in the same moment I wanted to believe the truth, so I chose to lean in and receive what Larry said. There was a moment of silence as I let the truth of his words sink in.

Then he shifted his strategy. Larry invited me to stand up. With a mixture of emotions, I surrendered to his love, sensing God was in this moment. He put his hands on my shoulder, looked me in the eyes, and pierced me again with the same statement. Boom! Another chunk of false belief removed.

Then he looked around the room and asked each man to bring the weight of their lives and their words to this battle for the truth to pierce my heart. Then as each man came, he took hold of my shoulders, looked into my eyes and, in his own way, spoke into my very being, "You belong in this room."

As their love and strength washed over me and within me, I thought, *Is this really happening? Wow. This is real. I can tell that these men are genuine. This is like the Council of Elrond in Lord of the Rings. Not only do I have friends, I have a group of strong men who believe in me. They see me as able. They see my change and are willing to relate to me as the new me. The real me. The free me. I will carry this experience for years to come. This moment is ammo against the enemy.*

The next day I wrote the following about the state of my heart:

Feelings: Safe because when the hunt of the enemy is strong in telling me that I'm a loser, that my life doesn't matter, and that no one cares, this moment will serve as a Memorial Stone of the day that concrete block blew up under the weight of the love, grace, and truth of Christ flowing through my brothers. Honored. Loved. Seen. Valuable. Grateful. Monumental. Free. Delighted in. Overwhelmed—almost too much to handle.

Desires fulfilled: To be included. To be a part. To have a place. To belong. To be safe.

Choices: To believe I do belong. I can be me and still have a place.

The beauty of wholehearted community is revealed when believers fiercely fight for one another's hearts and therefore act as the very body of Christ. Their words echo God's validating voice of love and truth. The ripple effect of that experience is that it is changing a man, a family, and even generations.

The Impact of God's Validation

What about you? As you reflect on God's validation of you through Creation, Redemption, Restoration, and the coming Consummation, what is happening in your heart? Where do you still struggle to believe that the Father loves you just like he does Jesus? That he is pleased with you, that he likes you and who you are becoming now and for all eternity?

When we consistently live confident in the Father's validation, we find freedom. The more we become rooted and grounded in experiencing our Father's love and joy, the more we become good and faithful daughters and sons who take risks in order to love deeply from the heart (see I Peter 1:22) and reveal God's glory throughout the earth. As we'll explore more fully in the next chapter, being grounded in God's love builds trust that empowers us to persevere in suffering, as Jesus did, for the joy set before us (see Hebrews 12:2).

FOR DEEPER CONNECTION

Personalize

Due to our sinful nature, as well as events in our past, we all struggle to some degree to believe we are truly loved. How does the truth that God has validated your identity as a beloved image bearer through Creation, Redemption, Restoration, and Consummation expand your understanding of his love for you?

Gain Awareness

How has your current experience or lack of experience of God's love and validation impacted the way you feel about yourself and God?

What would you like to change in the way you live now that would reflect a growing trust in God's love for and his delight in you?

Respond

Lord, thank you for demonstrating through creation, redemption, restoration, and the coming consummation the truth of your love for me. In those moments I'm tempted to doubt, remind me that I don't have to live under the burden of earning love, but can simply open my heart to receive it.

CHAPTER 11

No Pain Wasted

Broken down break through

Anisa

I sat in the shade of a large oak tree at a small monastery in north Alabama. It was the first full day of a four-day silent retreat. The lingering prayers of those who had sat there before me hung like a cloak around my shoulders. The breeze itself seemed to reverently whisper words of peace and rest. I could feel God present and my heart expectant. But first, I had to clear the air. I needed to be honest with him again about a source of long-held pain so I could focus on our time together.

I hate to bring this up again, Lord.

I feel like I always drag this into our conversations. I know I don't even have to speak it. You know what I'm going through. I've prayed this so many times.

For almost two decades, most of my marriage, my husband and I had prayed for God to provide the job he longed for in wildlife management, his field of study. It seemed this longing fit God's plan for us. But the break never came. At least not in the way we wanted. Instead of break*through*, it seemed like, in the years of unanswered prayers, everything had broken *down*. It was a shattering of my ideas of who God was, who I am, and what it looks like to walk in faith; the dismantling of my limited understanding of faith that God might rebuild on a foundation of truth and trust in his goodness.

But even though the prayers remained unanswered, over the past couple of years I had begun to see beauty in God remaking my beliefs. I came to trust God was good—not in the shallow soils of granted wishes but in the travail of finding God in dark and desperate places.

That morning under the oak, looking out at a still pond and feeling God around me, I only meant to clear the air. But in the silent reflection I heard him whisper one question: "What if the beauty of the work I'm doing in you is greater than the glory that would have been revealed if I had given you what you asked for?"

My breath caught as I tried to grasp what he said—that my life displayed God's glory in greater ways because of the pain. I was struck silent.

I felt the weightiness of this truth, of how my suffering was, as Paul says, "not worth comparing with the glory" God was revealing in me. How my life testified that God uses "all things" for good for those who love him and are called according to his purpose (see Romans 8:18–28).

That weekend, as I recalled all the tears, pleas, and bargains I'd offered, I felt God's comfort in the place of desires still unmet. I glimpsed his redemption of my pain, recognizing the way he grew my faith and taught me to trust him even when I didn't understand his ways. In that moment I felt loved, seen, and held.

Pain transforms us, in good ways or bad. And I've seen that when I've pressed into God in my pain, he has done good things in me. Unfortunately, too often our response to pain is to shut down our hearts, to disconnect not only from ourselves, but also from God and others. In this, we often miss how God longs to work in our pain.

I spoke with a spiritual director once who shared with me a portion of Jeremiah 51:58 where God is speaking about the Babylonians' coming judgment. The NIV translates the latter part of the verse "the peoples exhaust themselves for nothing, the nations' labor is only fuel for the flames." But Scottish theologian James Moffatt translates that same portion as "pagans waste their pains."[23]

Pagans waste their pains. . . . What a profoundly sad way to describe what we experience when we walk in independence from God. But the truth is, even believers can waste their pain. *If we don't allow*

God to work in the pain, redeeming it and bringing forth his glory and our good, all that suffering is wasted.

God's desired response from us in places of suffering is that we would choose open, vulnerable surrender to his love. Suffering gives us the opportunity to die to the Way of Pride and trust God for resurrection, life, and glory—if not in this life, then in the next. This is the truth God revealed to me as I sat beneath the oak reflecting on how my choice to walk in humility glorified God and produced life in me as I grew in trusting God's goodness. Trust increases our capacity to live vulnerably dependent on God, which, as David draws out in Psalm 8, is the key to defeating the work of Evil in our lives.

Our Vulnerable Dependence in Suffering Defeats the Enemy

Thousands of years ago, on a majestic star-filled night, David was captivated by the magnificence of God's creation. Overwhelmed by the sheer glory of the heavens, he could not help but worship:

> LORD, our Lord, how majestic is your name in all the earth! You have set your glory in the heavens....
>
> When I consider your heavens, the work of your fingers, the moon and the stars, which you have set in place, what is mankind that you are mindful of them, human beings that you care for them?
>
> You have made them a little lower than the angels and crowned them with glory and honor.
>
> You made them rulers over the works of your hands; you put everything under their feet. (Psalm 8:1, 3–6)

Written by David, this psalm offers a beautiful and poignant glimpse into the heart of a man after God's own heart. Thousands of years after they were penned, these words still resonate because they are an authentic expression of David's heart. His words reveal both his awestruck wonder and his sense of his own smallness in light of God's creation: "Who am I—who are we—that God would care for us? that he would send his Son for us?" It seems as if David is wrestling with his identity. What makes us so valuable that God would care for us? God answers through creation: God chose to make human beings "just a little lower than the angels." Then David, the one well acquainted with kings and crowns, remembers the majestic God who stooped down to crown us with glory and the honor of representing him throughout the earth. Now the transcendent glory of the majestic God of creation flows through the wellspring of the human heart.

In the midst of David's worship, though, verse 2 seems jarringly incongruous: "From the mouths of infants and nursing babies, you have established a stronghold on account of your adversaries in order to silence the enemy and the avenger" (Psalm 8:2 CSB).

What do infants, nursing babies, and adversaries have to do with contemplating the heavens and human beings crowned with glory and honor?

This verse reminds us that there is an adversary that seeks to diminish God's glory, particularly the glory of God in us. But David, a man known for his strength, a would-be king who pointed to the eternal King, conveys a shocking truth: it is not our strength but our dependence that disarms the enemy—the dependence of a baby.

Babies and toddlers fully rely on a loving, nurturing caregiver to meet their needs. The only control they have over their lives is the ability to cry out to the one entrusted with their care. This is the picture David paints of how God establishes a stronghold against the enemy. It is our vulnerable dependence on a loving God that silences the avenger. In some mysterious way, dependence is our strength. God's glory is displayed in our weakness.

The picture of a nursing baby captures one of the most intimate of human connections. And the image invites us into an equally intimate connection with the Father where we are strengthened and fed as we experience his love, his validation, and his delight in us. The enemy is powerless against that kind of dependence.

Generations after this psalm was written, God proved this truth when he sent the Son of David—Jesus—in the unlikeliest form: a dependent baby who grew to be a vulnerably dependent man who would forever silence the voice of the avenger. In the most significant moment in human history, Jesus opened himself to experience the full depravity of human beings, and, as he did, cried out, "My God, my God, why have you abandoned me?" (Matthew 27:46 NLT). Yet he still trusted the goodness of his Father to bring him through to resurrection, life, and glory.

Surrendering to God's Love in Suffering

Just as he was in Jesus' life and death, God is glorified when we yield our entire being in childlike trust and believe that he loves us even when circumstances seem to defy that belief. It took me twenty years before I was sitting under that oak tree in North Alabama and finally saw this truth. On the journey to that moment, two formative memories stand out: one in which God spoke clearly, and one in which he was silent.

As I shared in chapter 5, my childhood experiences led to a false visceral belief that if you have faith, prayer, and a little hard work, it will all work out. This belief came into play when it was time for my husband and me to transfer from community college to a four-year program. We listened to the advisor who shared with my husband that his chosen career in wildlife offered few job opportunities and even those were low paying.

"Don't worry about it," I told my husband. "Just do your best to make good grades. We'll pray about it, and God will open doors. It will all work out."

What I wouldn't give to go back and yank the words out of that girl's mouth. Many times over the next two decades my husband, in his pain and disappointment, wrestling with the concept of God's love, threw them back at me.

"You said it would all work out."

It did not all work out. And while not getting the job he wanted might not seem like a faith-shattering disappointment, it wasn't really about the job. It was about what not having that job communicated to him about God's love. It was about feeling unseen and unloved. It was about the pain of watching others get similar desires met. If God was good, if God was loving, why wouldn't he answer?

Ten years into this journey of walking beside my husband as he wrestled with his unmet desire for this job—the only one in the world he believed he was created for—I was struggling to read the Bible, to pray, to believe. After all, if God doesn't answer prayers, what's the use of praying?

One day, as I was lying on the couch, awash in self-pity, I told God all the harm I had experienced because he wasn't answering our prayers.

I feel like the stepchild at the back of the room waving to get your attention while all those you really care about are up front basking in your favor. Sure, I know you love me, but it's only because you have to. I'm just part of the human race that you collectively love. You don't really see me. I'm just an obligation.

Once a young girl who was fully confident in God's love, I was now a young adult living in a world of disappointment and pain, and I was struggling to believe God truly loved me.

And into that space God spoke: "The problem isn't that I haven't answered your prayers. The problem is that you have believed a lie."

Immediately, I knew it was true. I had allowed my experiences to shape how I viewed God's love. I agreed with the lies of the enemy who wanted me to distrust God's love in hard circumstances. The pain I experienced, the lack of connection to God, wasn't because God had moved away from me but because I, embracing a lie, had moved away from him.

That was a pivotal moment as God began illuminating other areas where I was operating out of false beliefs that kept me from fully experiencing his love. He started me on a journey toward the understanding that truth is truth regardless of circumstances. God's love is not evidenced by how or when he answers my prayers.

But, as we've discussed, it is not enough to know truth only at a rational level. We must know it at a whole heart level. And it takes time to close that disconnect between our rational and visceral knowing of truth. I continued for the next several years to wrestle with trusting God's love when my experiences didn't feel loving. I longed to become anchored in God's love so circumstances couldn't toss me about like an unmoored ship. During this time, my husband's pain from ongoing disappointment pushed me to the end of what I thought I could endure. It impacted every area of our lives—the way we related to each other as well as the degree to which he was able to engage with our kids on days when he vacillated between discouragement and anger.

On one of those days, I sat curled up on the bathroom floor, wracked with sobs, again pouring out my heart to God about my own pain.

Can't you see how we are struggling?

Don't you care about the harm our children are experiencing with two parents who can't find their footing?

Can't you see how much glory you would receive if you would just answer our prayers? I would tell everyone about how faithful you are.

And God was silent.

And that felt unendurable.

In that season when God felt distant, I clung to scriptural promises such as Isaiah 43:2. As I reflected in my journal:

> God whispered in my ear that the waters would not overtake me even though it felt like I was drowning.

That promise was like a life preserver offering comfort in the raging storm.

In that place where I often felt alone, unseen, and uncared for, I kept going back to those convicting words about believing a lie, torn between biblical truth and what felt true based on circumstances. When doubts surfaced, I held tight to scripture. I shared with friends and family who gave me courage to stay in the battle for my heart. And I chose not to agree with the false belief that God did not love or care for me.

In the days and years that followed, I chose God's truth again and again and again. As I did, I felt my heart begin to open more fully to experience God's comfort in the loss, and gradually my once-shaken confidence in God became a gut-level trust in his love and goodness. The weight of this unmet longing for God to answer my husband's prayer the way we wanted it answered began to lift. At times my heart is still tender as we live with the pain of unfulfilled dreams. But in that tenderness, I continue to turn to God for comfort, no longer acting as if I am that overlooked stepchild outside God's favor. I increasingly rest, instead, in knowing I am loved.

In this season, my community was a significant source of encouragement. When I felt disconnected from God, I had people in my life who served as channels of his love. They saw me, listened to me, empathized with me, and spoke truth to me:

"I know this is painful and deep. And my heart hurts with you for that."

"My heart breaks for all you are having to navigate, but I am in awe of how well you are walking through this. It speaks deeply of your years of working to understand your own heart and becoming more aware of God's heart for you."

These godly friends sat with me in the pain and validated it. When I couldn't see God working in my situation, I could see his faithfulness in their lives, and it gave me courage to hold on in faith, to choose trust.

In those years of pressing into God in hard places, God exposed other lies and, as I repented, he began purifying my desires so my desire to reveal his glory became greater than my deceptive desire for my own comfort.

God brings forth beauty from the ashes of suffering (see Isaiah 61:3), but lacking that vision, we often move away from pain or deny its existence and sabotage the good God has for us—the deeper intimacy that awaits as we experience his love *in suffering*. Just as gold is refined by fire and diamonds are crystallized when subjected to intense heat and pressure, God's glory in us becomes more radiant as we mature through suffering. This kind of refining has led me to have greater trust in God's love and, in turn, greater freedom from fear and the courage I need to accept God's invitation to co-create beauty through writing. In prior chapters we touched on our heart questions related to our desires for intimacy, identity, and purpose.

Another heart question, though, flows out of desire to experience love. In fact, everything we believe hinges on this question: Is God trustworthy?

We touched in prior chapters on our shared questions and desires connected to intimacy, identity, and purpose which are vital to our experience of fullness of life.

As it relates to God, though, there is another heart question that flows out of our desire to experience love—one upon which everything we believe hinges: Is God trustworthy?

How we answer that question determines the extent to which we experience divine intimacy, identity, and purpose because, as mentioned earlier, trust is the valve that opens our heart to the aquifer of God's love. When I subconsciously answered the question about God's trustworthiness with no and struggled to trust his goodness in my pain, that choice came with a cost: lack of intimacy with God. Because identity is formed in the context of our relationship with God and others who are designed to reveal God to us, I in turn struggled with understanding my identity which impacted my ability to fulfill my purpose as God's image bearer.

Human suffering—including yours and mine—is the area where we are most susceptible to the enemy's attack on our beliefs about God's trustworthiness.

In her book *Prayer in the Night*, Tish Harrison Warren says the problem of pain is that it is "the engine of our grimmest doubts. It can sometimes wither belief altogether."[24]

Warren cites a survey showing the most commonly stated reason for unbelief among Millennials and Gen Zers was being unable to reconcile how a good God could allow evil and suffering. What we long for, she says, is "a God who notices our suffering, who cares enough to act, and who will make all things new."[25]

And that's part of the problem of suffering. We know this world is not as it should be. We live with an awareness of what will one day be restored but are tethered to a time and place that has not yet been made fully new. Part of trusting that God's heart is good is believing he will one day make all things new.

Suffering sets up a battle. Will we look beyond what we now see, to God's goodness, and gain courage, or will we be overwhelmed with the suffering, give up, and lose heart?

This is what Paul says is our hope:

> Therefore we do not lose heart. Though outwardly we are wasting away, yet inwardly we are being renewed day by day. For our light and momentary troubles are achieving for us an eternal glory that far outweighs them all. So we fix our eyes not on what is seen, but on what is unseen, since what is seen is temporary, but what is unseen is eternal. (2 Corinthians 4:16–18)

To "lose heart" in this context is to become weary or lose courage. But Paul points out that we are strengthened when we fix our eyes on the eternal glory that God is bringing forth from our suffering.

In suffering, God reveals the truth of our hearts. He brings to light the places where we are still entangled by our self-protective strategies, the ways we try to meet our desires apart from him. He illuminates places of fear, distrust, and pride that we may be refined as we surrender to the ongoing work of Christ in us.

The Redemptive Work of Christ Through You

The change that comes as we choose the Way of Humility in suffering isn't limited to our lives. As God's glory overflows through the wellspring of our hearts, it offers life to others. As Paul explains, "For we who are alive are always being given over to death for Jesus' sake, so that his life may also be revealed in our mortal body. So then, death is at work in us, but life is at work in you" (2 Corinthians 4:11–12).

This is part of the redemption of our pain, knowing that in dying to our fallen self and the Way of Pride, we bring life to others. I'm grateful for those around me who have chosen to trust God's goodness in their pain. Through their testimonies, I gain courage to persevere in hard places, trusting that God will, in his time and way, bring forth glory.

We cannot choose a life free from suffering. But we can choose how we walk through pain and, in part, the extent to which we experience God redeeming our pain and using it for his glory.

Which way will you choose? Will you choose to look beyond your light and momentary afflictions to see the incomparable weight of glory (see 2 Corinthians 4:16–18)? Or will you lose heart and seek the expediency of meeting your deep desires in your time and way?

Evil tempts us to walk in the Way of Pride, seeking our own glory. God offers a vision of earth filled with radiant glory and invites us to be part of his display of glory now and for all eternity (See Habakkuk 2:14, John 17:22-23). To be part of this display of glory, we must choose the Way of Humility. As we do, our suffering can give way to breakthroughs that enable us to experience resurrection, life, and glory.

FOR DEEPER CONNECTION

Personalize

How do you typically respond to pain and suffering?

Gain Awareness

What does your response reveal about the true state of your heart (positive or negative)?

What do you most desire from God when you are in pain and suffering?

Respond

Loving Father, I confess that in my deepest pain my desire for rescue can outweigh my desire to choose your will and way. When my broken heart and world weigh heavy, it can be hard to trust that anything in my circumstances can be used for good. Help me to see the glory beyond the pain, the glory of being increasingly conformed to the image of Christ. Comfort me that I might extend comfort to others in their own places of pain.

CHAPTER 12

God Doesn't Set You Up for Failure

Embracing repentance and mourning to become who you're created to be

Anisa

Around twenty years ago, when my husband and I became involved with Wellspring Group and started our journey to becoming wholehearted people, it was messy. If you'd asked my advice at the time, I'd have said, "I 100 percent do not recommend trying to engage from a whole heart with your spouse."

When my husband first attended the Battle for the Heart Retreat, he began understanding more of what was going on in his heart. As he shared those revelations, our conversations seemed to turn into a never-ending discussion around the things I was doing that were hurtful or negatively impacting him. None of what he said was mean-spirited—he was trying to draw us closer by inviting deeper, more authentic conversation. But it left me feeling raw and exposed as, for the first time in our relationship, I had to face the ways I wasn't loving him well.

Looking back, now, on nearly two decades of deep heart work, what I've discovered about living wholeheartedly—in the context of family relationships, friendships, and work—is that our capacity to build and live in wholehearted community is based on the extent to which we are willing to embrace humility. And embracing a life of humility requires us to face our brokenness, including the ways we fail to love others well.

Facing my own brokenness—or my tendency to choose the Way of Pride—has probably been, for me, the most difficult part of living in wholehearted community because it carries an element of pain and sometimes shame. However, the more I experience God's love and validation for who I am as his beloved child, the more I can trust his goodness to comfort me in the pain and to free me from shame.

I've realized I cannot be the person God created me to be unless I honestly face the ways I have sinned against God and others—causing pain—and acknowledge the pain and suffering I've experienced through no fault of my own. This is suffering that comes at the hands of others or from living in a fallen world.

As I've **faced the ways I've sinned,** including the ways I've chosen independence from God to avoid suffering or to meet my own desires, I've had to recognize the cost, then wholeheartedly repent and mourn.

As I've **faced the ways I've been sinned against,** I've had to wholeheartedly mourn and forgive.

In the vulnerability of repentance and mourning, I've opened my heart to more fully receive God's comfort, freeing me from guilt and shame and empowering me to build deeper, more authentic connections with God and others. This has made embracing the pain worth it.

Now we return to Abby's story to see a painfully beautiful picture of wholehearted repentance, mourning, and godly comfort coming together to draw her deeper into God's love, her true identity, and divine purpose.

Embracing Repentance and the Beauty of God's Design

In chapter 8 we shared about the work God did in Abby that led to her husband and her adopting three daughters. In 2020, God called her to step into Wellspring Group's new position of managing director and to oversee daily operations.

Along the way, the men and women in her community protected and propelled her into her part in the Larger Story by calling out her glory—the glory of God's image in her—and challenging her distortions—those things that stopped the flow of God's glory through her. These distortions included false gut-level beliefs she had to acknowledge, own, and repent of to be the woman God created her to be. As she recalls,

> In spring 2020, when our then-managing director resigned, he shared with me his recommendation to the board that I replace him—and he boldly, convincingly called out a glory in me that I never knew existed.
>
> "Abby, you are the managing director," he said. "It's in you. You have Larry's trust. I'm just recommending the board see what I see in you."
>
> The timing of this change aligned in a way that was divinely orchestrated. Over the previous six months, I had grappled with God about his calling on my life. I was trying to understand my purpose in light of who God uniquely created me to be.
>
> When I say grappled, I should clarify. I mean argued, resisted, denied, and minimized what I sensed he was saying because I struggled to believe I could be the woman he was revealing me to be. In many ways, I relate more to a desire to be safe and small. But when God opened the door to move into the position of managing director, I knew God had been preparing me to say yes.

With her new position, Abby carried significant responsibility not only for finding solutions to the new reality of family life and ministry, but also for emotionally supporting children and adults whose lives had changed drastically overnight. At times it was overwhelming. Abby was forced to recognize major disconnects between what she rationally knew about God's love for her and what she believed deep within about God's heart toward her.

She first became aware of this new area of internal disconnect through a dream. In that dream, she was in a classroom being tested on something she had not been prepared for. As she processed the dream, she recognized her heart belief that God was testing her and setting her up to fail:

> I was certain God had set me up for failure in more ways than one. I believed he had called me into the roles of organizational leader and mother, but both roles seemed impossibly difficult. I was destined to fail. I felt like I was constantly trying to catch up to what was expected of me. I often joked with my girls, "You've been children longer than I've been a mother. I'm trying to catch up to you." And it seemed as though all my equipping in accounting and financial planning didn't add up to what was needed for leading people in a ministry built around living from a whole heart.

The disconnection God revealed in Abby was rooted in a childhood belief that it was up to her to hold everything together for everyone around her. If she could achieve this, she believed she would experience the peace and rest she longed for.

> How this played out in adulthood was an underlying message that if anyone was disrupted, unsettled, disappointed, or in pain, then I have somehow failed.

Though Abby longed to be the woman God created her to be, she also deeply desired peace and rest—two things which seemed at odds with co-leading a family and ministry through the pain and disruption of a global pandemic.

James refers to this experience of battling desires:

> What causes fights and quarrels among you? Don't they come from your desires that battle within you? You desire but do not have, so you kill. You covet, but you cannot get what you want, so you quarrel and fight. You do not have because you do not ask God. When you ask, you do not receive, because you ask

with wrong motives, that you may spend what you get on your pleasures. (James 4:1–3)

Abby responded to her battling desires by taking on a distorted sense of responsibility for keeping those around her stable. She pursued the deceptive desire for control as she tried to predict, prevent, and protect others from stress and emotional disruption so she could experience peace and rest. For example, within the ministry, she found herself playing peacekeeper, avoiding conflict instead of moving into it. This sabotaged her desire to love well as she failed to effectively challenge others for their growth and for everyone's good.

As Abby further processed her dream, God led her to Luke 22:31–32, "Simon, Simon, Satan has asked to sift all of you as wheat. But I have prayed for you, Simon, that your faith may not fail."

When she read this verse, Abby had a clear sense that the Lord was preparing her for Evil's attempt to sift her. She also heard the Father's reassurance: "I am not testing you. I have given you everything you need for this moment. I am with you."

Within two weeks of the dream and God's revelation through scripture, Abby had to draw upon God's promise in a season of suffering more intense than anything she had previously experienced as she walked through relational fallout within close community.

> The experience of rejection, violation of values, misunderstanding, and being misunderstood was overwhelming and disorienting.
>
> I was convinced I had failed as a mother, as a friend, and more importantly, as an image bearer. There was such a sense of shame. I just kept saying over and over, "I have failed. I have failed." Ultimately, I believed I had failed God.

As things continued to spiral outside Abby's control, she reached a breaking point one Friday.

> All day and all night, I grieved the pain of the broken relationships, of feeling like a failure.

And then, at the place of my deepest pain, I realized I had a choice in how I wanted to respond to the suffering. Finally, in that place of despair, I told God: *If I lose everything, if I lose everyone, I believe you are enough and that your heart is good.*

I repented of the belief that God had set me up for failure. I chose to believe his heart was good. I could trust his purposes.

As I faced the truth of what I believed, I also had to face the cost of my unbelief to me, to God, and to those around me. I saw how I had pained God by diminishing his call on my life, by not trusting his goodness, and, at times, despising who he had created me to be.

Something shifted when I began to see my resistance was rejection of him as well as rejection of me as his creation and of the giftings he had purposefully placed in me. I was broken when I realized I had traded the truth of the Creator and who he created me to be and chosen to believe the lie from the enemy that I was not enough, that the call was too great.

All I could do was repent of the lies I had believed about God and myself and mourn. I grieved the pain I had caused my heavenly Father when I rejected him and his truth. I grieved all I had lost by not believing God's goodness and instead judging myself so harshly for nearly forty years. And then I grieved the loss of who I could have been and how I could have offered more to the people I love. Then, as I opened my heart to receive God's grace, I experienced his comfort.

Notice what was going on in Abby as she began to repent at a wholeheart level:

Thoughts: Abby had to recognize her desires and how she'd tried to meet them by controlling people and circumstances; recognize the disconnection between her visceral beliefs and biblical truth; and face the cost of her self-protective strategies stemming from lack of trust.

Desires: Owning her desires freed her to then open her heart to the ways God wanted to meet her desires.

Feelings: As Abby recognized the cost of her sin, she allowed herself to feel the weight of her choices and mourn.

Choices: As Abby recognized her sin, she chose the Way of Humility: she repented and moved toward God to experience his love and comfort. She chose to trust that God was enough and that his heart toward her was good.

We see in Abby's story how repentance and mourning go hand in hand to bring us back to fullness and to restore us to right relationship with God, ourselves, and others. God calls us to repent, but we must also recognize our need to appropriately grieve the pain our sin has caused.

The pain we cause ourselves often expresses itself as shame or guilt. Left unresolved, this pain can block intimacy as shame leads us to hide and isolate. In hiding we cannot fully know ourselves or be known. In Abby's case, mourning opened her heart to intimacy, to the blessing of God's comforting presence.

As Matthew reminds us, "Blessed are those who mourn, for they will be comforted" (5:4).

When Abby turned to God in humility, she experienced him meeting her, drawing her out of mourning and into deeper experiences of his love, grace, and truth.

> As I was able to surrender to God's love—to open my heart to believe he truly loved me and that he did not set me up for failure—and to mourn the cost of the lies I had believed and how I had fallen short of revealing his glory, I was able to move into wholehearted repentance. I took responsibility and owned my part, while also letting go of things I was not responsible for. There were points where I struggled with shame and choose to draw near to God. But as I did, I experienced him meeting me and bringing healing and redemption.

The impact of this change was significant. I began to talk to God differently and ask him, "What is it you want me to reveal of you in this situation?" instead of believing that I shouldn't be the one there in the first place!

Abby's wholehearted repentance followed the path James lays out for us:

> Submit yourselves, then, to God. Resist the devil, and he will flee from you. Come near to God and he will come near to you. Wash your hands, you sinners, and purify your hearts, you double-minded. Grieve, mourn and wail. Change your laughter to mourning and your joy to gloom. Humble yourselves before the Lord, and he will lift you up. (James 4:7–10)

The double mindedness James speaks of is that of being divided in interest between the things of God and things of the world. James calls us to recognize where our thoughts and desires don't line up with God's, to allow ourselves to experience the full weight of the emotions that come as we repent of seeking our own way, and to allow God to purify our desires so we want what he wants and choose what he chooses.

Turning from sinful behavior and beginning to embrace God's desires for us is hard. In Abby's story we see two elements critical for moving into that kind of wholehearted repentance:

- She **discovered the energy that fueled her sin**, the deceptive desires that drove her behavior.
- She **discovered the energy for change** when she recognized what was at stake: she wanted to be the woman God created her to be.

Energy for change comes from pain and gain.

As we've stated previously, desires drive our choices. When we get in touch with the deep desires behind our actions, we can choose differently. In Abby's case, her desires for peace and rest drove her to the deceptive desire for *control* in hopes of gaining peace and rest. As her self-protective strategies fell apart, she recognized the cost to God, herself, and others, and she repented.

Through repentance, Abby recognized that her desire to be the woman God created her to be was deeper than her fear-driven desire for control. This desire energized her to choose to trust God's heart that she might be a woman who increasingly revealed his glory. As she did, her desire for peace and rest didn't go away, but they have been increasingly purified, and she is experiencing peace in being who she is created to be. This has brought rest as she's released the weight of the responsibility for making everyone happy.

God convicts us of our sin and invites us into the Way of Humility and reconnection with him and others. As we respond in vulnerability by opening our hearts and repenting, we experience God's love, grace, and truth in greater measure. This deepening experience of love empowers us to increasingly live from our identity and purpose as beloved image bearers.

Godly Mourning

In Abby's story we see how repentance and mourning are intertwined. The same can also be true when we have been sinned against. When we mourn what we have suffered due to the choices of others, God often illuminates ways we have sinned as we've tried to protect ourselves. This revelation of the part we have played in our own pain leads us to repentance.

However, other times, such as when a loved one dies or when we suffer significant disappointment, it is appropriate, even necessary, to simply mourn.

Many people fear mourning, believing if they open the manhole covering their pain, they'll find a black hole they'll never return from. And it is true that grieving can feel overwhelming at times. In some cases, you may need others in the Body of Christ to journey with you, to build you up as you heal and get back onto a solid and secure landing in your faith. This is what godly community is intended to do (Ephesians 4:11–13). At other times we may need the help of someone gifted with the skills and knowledge to safely guide us through the process. Abby's journey of repentance meant facing intense suffering and pain as God exposed multiple threads of her self-protective strategies. Yet he drew her into deepening experiences of repentance in order to strengthen her trust that his heart toward her was good. As she shares,

> My journey through that period involved countless hours of engaging in wholehearted community, heart-wrenching conversations with God, and guided direction through an extremely gifted and anointed therapist.

Repentance and mourning are not things we should occasionally do but are spiritual disciplines we should continuously practice as we become aware of ways we have sinned or been sinned against.

The disciplines of repentance and mourning help us catch potential heart blockages before they become dams blocking God's love to and through us. We live in a fallen world, and none of us escapes without scars. For some, they are like deep grooves in our hearts, seemingly permanent reminders of the violations we have suffered. Mourning and repentance open our hearts to the healing balm of God's love.

How should we respond when we are sinned against?

First, you must let go of what is not yours to own—what is not your fault. You are not responsible for the ways others have sinned against you. As I mentioned earlier, what you are responsible for is the way you have responded out of pride and independence rather than surrender and trust.

If we choose the Way of Pride when we encounter pain, Evil tempts us to shut down and withdraw or to angrily try to dominate and control. This leads to disconnection from:

- our hearts, as we fail to face what has been done to us by denying, repressing, minimizing, or medicating our pain;
- God's heart, as we close ourselves off from the healing comfort he longs to offer; and
- others, as we hold back from repairing the relationship, when appropriate, and build barriers to prevent people from drawing near to spare ourselves from future pain.

In the Way of Humility, God invites us to face the pain and appropriately mourn that we might receive comfort. This leads to increasing connection with:

- our hearts, as we, in self-compassion, acknowledge the impact of the violation, validate rather than dismiss our feelings and desires, open our hearts to receive God's comfort, and choose how to respond based on the man or woman we long to be and God desires us to be;
- God's heart, as we open ourselves to receive his comforting love and compassion; and
- others, as we remain appropriately open to those God has placed in our lives to be a channel of his love, grace, and truth in our suffering.

A life of intimate connection where God's love empowers us to live from our true identity and purpose is part of the resurrection, life, and glory we experience when we die to our own will and way. As we choose to turn to God, in humility, we can trust that he will be faithful to lift us up (James 4:10), to increasingly conform us to his image that we might become the man or woman he created us to be. In the words of C.S. Lewis,

> The more we let God take us over, the more truly ourselves we become—because He made us. He invented us. He invented all the different people that you and I were intended to be…It is when I turn to Christ, when I give myself up to his personality, that I first begin to have a real personality of my own.[26]

Abby's journey was a three-year period of both suffering and surrendering to God, of repentance and mourning. But she came to be—as Lewis wrote—"more truly" herself. God was preparing her, his beloved image bearer, for something bigger than her 2020 self could have imagined. In January 2024 Abby became Wellspring Group's executive director. Reflecting on God's preparation, she shares,

> During this multiyear journey in the wilderness, the Lord pursued me and reframed my understanding of who he created me to be. This process built resiliency and gave me confidence to step into the next season.

What about you? Does Abby's story encourage you to wonder what God's invitation to you is today? Could he be calling you into deeper places of repentance and mourning so that you might become "more truly" yourself?

Repentance and mourning are about more than just facing your brokenness. They're about surrendering to the love of a relentlessly pursuing Father who longs for you to be free to be the human being he has created, redeemed, and is restoring you to be.

FOR DEEPER CONNECTION

Personalize

What has been your experience of repentance and mourning?

Gain Awareness

What might it feel like to repent and grieve while trusting that God loves you and is for your good?

What desire would it satisfy to consistently live with this level of vulnerability and humility, trusting that even in your brokenness you are loved?

Respond

Gracious Heavenly Father, thank you for not only forgiving my sin but for covering my shame. In my brokenness, it's easy to lose sight of your love and to fail to love well. Open my eyes to the ways I've sinned and chosen the Way of Pride. In the experiences where I've been sinned against, please meet me in my pain with the healing balm of your comfort.

CHAPTER 13

Dare to Risk

Becoming who you are created to be, together

Anisa

How did I get here?

That's the question I'm asking as I write this last chapter.

As I think back and remember parts of my journey that led to this book, I see my teen and young adult self with a vibrant, though untested faith. I felt deeply loved by God and obeyed out of my love for him. I experienced unity in the sense that doing for God flowed from being with God. But in my twenties and thirties, when it seemed every day brought a new challenge, I began to lose heart, to lose myself. I still loved God, but my relationship with him became more compartmentalized, relegated to time spent reading the Bible or praying. I didn't connect as easily to his love—even doubted it at times—so doing for God no longer flowed from love but from a sense of duty. And dutiful faith did not bring the fullness of life I longed for.

In my late thirties, I reconnected to my heart and to God's heart, and he began exposing the lies I subconsciously believed that had kept me from experiencing his love. I began a journey back to my true self—someone who loves colorful socks, who enjoys thinking deep thoughts, and who is fulfilled when I share them with others through writing.

In my earliest childhood dreams, writing held a place in my future. When I wasn't reading stories, I created them in my head. I still remember my first "published" piece, *The Family Weekly*—a small, handwritten, photocopied, and personally-delivered accounting of our family's adventures. Available for the bargain price of a quarter. I still have a few copies in dusty boxes in a closet, along with scribbled poems and, I think, maybe even a school paper or two I was particularly fond of.

I majored in journalism but decided just a few months into my short-lived career that I didn't enjoy writing about others' misfortunes. I wanted to tell stories that moved people, ones that had meaning and didn't intrude on another's grief. So, I switched jobs, and years passed. Every now and then, the writer in me would peek her head out from the mountain of responsibilities and make herself known. But mostly, I went about the business of living. And dying. Maybe not in the literal sense but looking back now on those years where I shut down parts of my heart—slowly dying to my true self—one of the casualties was my ability to dream; another was to create.

But around 2018, I became aware of an increasing desire to be creative. For two years I prayed, asking God to give me the ability to create. I knew God was a creator. And because I've been made in his image, I felt there had to be within me an ability to create. But what that might look like, I had no clue, until God spoke to me: "This is how you create—through writing."

Oh, yeah. I remember that part of me.

Around the time of that revelation, in 2020, through mutual prayer and discernment among our team, God opened an unexpected door. I was offered a new position on staff, that of Creative Director, and invited to be part of this book project.

As I reflected on that time in my journal, I wrote about feeling undone, like "a thawing iceberg with a tsunami of feelings cascading all around." I realized I had been living as a shadow of the person I was created to be, but God was inviting me to "cast off the pale imitation of who I was" so I could more fully become the woman he created me to be.

This process of more fully becoming who I'm uniquely created to be—one who creates beauty through writing—required ever increasing levels of walking in the Way of Humility. When I imagined, in younger years, writing a book, I feared the vulnerability of pouring my heart into something that could be rejected. I thought to hide under the safety of a pseudonym. So, the initial thought that I would help Larry write his story felt comfortable. But three years into the process, Larry sensed God leading him to invite me to become his coauthor. I had to choose: would I be willing to step out, in vulnerability, in my own voice, and tell more of my story? Could I stay grounded in God's love, trusting that my part in God's Larger Story is simply to be an offering, even if what I offer is rejected?

And even beyond stepping out, could I dare believe I could be the person God created me to be?

Perhaps nothing describes it better than this journal entry from April 2021:

> "Beautiful girl, you were created to do great things."
>
> Those words are inscribed on the outer edge of a bracelet I bought for my daughter this past Christmas. When I saw it on a Facebook ad in December, she immediately came to mind, and I thought: *This is how I see you. This is what I want you to believe about yourself. You have so much to offer. If you could just see yourself the way I see you . . .*
>
> Yesterday my husband reminded me of Moses when God called him to lead the children of Israel into freedom, and he questioned God, *Who am I that I could do this great thing?* As I processed what my husband said, I realized that I could identify with Moses questioning God. Recently God has opened some doors that require stepping out and taking risks. In that stretching, I struggle with believing I can be who he created me to be, do what he created me to do.
>
> Then God whispered to me the same words I longed for my daughter to believe: "Beautiful girl, you were created to do great things."
>
> *You talkin' to me, God? I'm just an ordinary girl from south Alabama surrounded by ordinary people from south Alabama. I'm lookin' around. I don't see no one else you seem to be talkin' to. But, seriously, you talkin' to me?*

I've been in various meetings over the past few weeks and months, and my sense that God has Wellspring Group on the cusp of something great grows stronger and stronger. In moments, I'm amazed that God would place my story smack dab in the middle of it all. It's humbling. And a little bit scary.

Yesterday I was in the little bit scary place. Taking a walk to talk it through with the Lord, I thought about the bracelet.

I wondered, *How can I teach any of my daughters to believe they can do great things if I don't fully believe it of myself?* It's not that I completely *dis*believe I can be that person. It's that there comes a moment when you have to fully embrace who God says you can be, then take the first fumbling steps in that direction. But when each step takes me to a place of greater vision of the Story before me, it's hard not to shrink back and think, *God, you've got the wrong girl.*

That's when he whispered again:

Beautiful girl.
Beautiful, beautiful girl.
YOU.
WERE CREATED.
To do.
GREAT THINGS.
THIS is how I see you.
THIS is how I long for you to see yourself.
Beautiful, beautiful girl.

With all the understanding of a mother's heart for her daughter, I experienced my Father expressing his longing for me to believe this of myself.

Yet, part of me always wants to shrink back at any hint of greatness within myself. I fear it. It seems risky. Unsafe.

Me? Are you talkin' to me?

As I read those words four years later, I realize God answered my questions about my identity—*Could I be the woman he created me to be?*—through wholehearted community. He reassured me through promises of his presence in scripture. Family and friends called out my glory—the image of God they saw uniquely displayed in my life. They prayed for me and challenged me never to settle for less than all God has for me. They were echoes of God's voice affirming who I am and what I am created for.

But what are the great things God created each of us for?

Greatness is the courage to simply be who God has created us to be. We are recipients of his love, who are to love wherever we are. In the car line, at the grocery store, at work, in the neighborhood. A hundred times daily you have the opportunity for greatness because a hundred times daily you have the opportunity to display God's glory.

I remember, as a freshman in college, walking past our dorm kitchen with a sink full of dirty dishes when I felt the Lord gently nudge me to love my fellow students by cleaning the dishes. Not mention it, not draw attention to myself, just do it because it pleased him. I did it joyfully. Until today, that act remained hidden.

Why mention it now? Because many of us look around our ordinary lives in ordinary communities and feel rather ordinary. We view the "great things" God calls human beings to as being reserved for those who are more intelligent, more talented, more ambitious than we are. We think there is no greatness within us.

But we'd be wrong, because my simple act of love from a daughter to her Father, on behalf of a dorm of girls who'd never know how I'd loved them, was no less great than writing a book or leading a company or painting the Sistine Chapel or whatever else our concept of greatness entails. That moment was just as fulfilling as any I've ever experienced because I was with God, expressing my love to him, giving love to others, even knowing it would remain unseen and unreciprocated. It was me, being who I'm called to be, doing the thing God called me to do on a very ordinary day on a very ordinary college campus. That was greatness. And in that, God was glorified.

God glorified. Through you. Through me. Isn't that—as the Westminster Shorter Catechism so eloquently states it—the "chief end of man": "to glorify God, and to enjoy him forever"?[27]

As we've journeyed together, Larry and I hope you've seen more clearly how *you* glorify God just by being who you are. Becoming wholehearted is not about doing more things *for* God but about being more *with* God in every moment, every step—even in the most ordinary things you do.

With God. Heart-to-heart. As you live increasingly connected to your heart, God's heart, and the hearts of others, choosing the Way of Humility, God restores you to the glory and honor he planned for you from Creation. You are becoming the person you're created to be—someone who experiences God's love, lives as one who is loved, and has the courage to love. You are fulfilling your purpose and God's desire for you to reveal his glory among the earth. This is the experience of divine intimacy, identity, and purpose that is the fullness of life you long for.

Yet, even as we taste that fullness on earth, we will not experience it perfectly until eternity. Still, we press on. We fight "the good fight" as we finish the race (2 Timothy 4:7). That "good fight" is the fight for our own hearts while cooperating with God in our restoration, but it's also fighting for the hearts of others. We hope you've seen the personal impact of living in deep, authentic community woven through all the stories we've shared. Heart-to-heart. Impacting and being impacted as we both give and receive divine love.

This is our vision for wholehearted community: wholehearted believers who come together to experience and express God's love to him, one another, and the world. Creating community that is a place of acceptance and challenge, of rejoicing and mourning, of shared burdens where together we know the love of Christ that surpasses knowledge—that we may be filled with all the fullness of God overflowing to his glory (see Ephesians 3:19–21).

Looking Back

Larry

Fifty-two years ago, as a freshman in college, I first glimpsed the captivating vision of the glory of God in community. God kept growing that vision, particularly in 2003 through my twelve days of prayer and fasting and summer grad school experience.

As I look back, I see a lot of pain, broken expectations, loss, betrayal, failure, disappointment, and disillusionment. I see a lot of hard, courageous choices Mary and I made, a lot of mistakes, and some regrets. Sometimes I wonder if it's worth all the effort, particularly when I see the brokenness of my life, of the Body of Christ, and the pain caused by fallen leaders.

But then I remember the eternal moments like beholding the glory of God in a coffee shop with Rob and Bryan. I remember countless moments in small groups where we opened our broken, vulnerable hearts to God and to one another—and, in some mysterious way, God consumed our living sacrifice with the fire of his glory.

I remember stories like Robby's—where we saw, heard, felt, and touched the love, grace, and truth of Christ revealed through his body. I recall marriages and families being transformed as children experience parents becoming wholehearted and changing the course for future generations; organizational leaders like Bryan building environments where the people they lead and serve can actually flourish as human beings; pastors courageously inviting their people into the messiness of wholehearted community, freeing them to experience fullness of life; missionaries being restored to the hope and healing of the gospel for themselves and for those they long to reach with the love of Christ.

As I pause to remember, I see the faces of these people now and in eternity. I see you. I long for you to know that wherever you are on your path to becoming wholehearted, there is hope that you can become the person God created you to be and that you long to be.

I long for you to deeply believe that you and your heart are worth fighting for and that in some way, God has come to you through this book.

Then, I see the face of God shining upon me, smiling upon me. I see a teenage boy dreaming of greatness, of being all I could be by giving myself to a captivating vision and doing it with other people committed to that same vision. Now, close to the end of life, I realize that greatness is simply found in the lifelong adventure of letting go of Larry the Achiever and becoming Larry the Beloved. This is who I am. In the pain and joy of being loved, I have discovered my true purpose: to be loved and, out of the overflow, create opportunities for people to encounter the presence of Christ in community. This is the fullness of life I've longed for. Yet there is more.

I see the joy set before me as I grow ever closer to that day when I pass into eternity to see and hear my heavenly Father's voice, "Well done, good and faithful son, enter into my joy." To glimpse his smile now, to taste that joy now, and to anticipate its fullness in eternity makes the battle, the pain, and the scars all worth it.

Larry and Anisa

It has been a long journey getting to where we are today, offering you these final words. We have navigated significant personal challenges, withstood devastatingly painful attacks from Evil, and cooperated with God in our own restoration journeys to do the great things he has called us to do.

We are different in age, gender, temperament, and experience, but God brought us together to bring forth something larger than ourselves: to give you a glimpse of what life can be when we risk walking in the Way of Humility—connecting to our own hearts, to one another's hearts, and, most of all, to God's heart. We see more clearly now the truth of what we wrote in chapter 2, that together, in community with God and one another, we more fully reveal God.

We've sought to work together on this book in such a way that his heart, his love, would flow freely to one another and ultimately to your open, vulnerable heart. We hope we have loved you well as we've vulnerably opened our hearts and stories to you.

We could not have completed this book without a deep conviction of the Father's love for you, his smile over you, his delight in you. So, as we've considered what we most want to communicate in our final moments together, our deepest longing is for you to know that in Christ, the same words the Father spoke to his Son, the Father speaks to you:

"You are my child, whom I love; with you I am well pleased."

And that is as good as it gets!

Next Steps

We are honored that you have walked with us down the path to becoming wholehearted through connection with God's heart, your heart, and the hearts of others. Along the way, we considered three essential questions:

- Am I loved?
- Who am I?
- Why am I here?

Now you may be asking another question: How? How do we live this out day by day?

As we sought to share authentically, the path to becoming wholehearted is worth it, but it is not easy. It requires continually dying to the Way of Pride and choosing the Way of Humility—trusting that God will bring forth his glory in this life or the next. A significant step in becoming wholehearted involves surrendering our whole hearts to his love in community.

As you reflect on your next steps on the path to becoming who God created you to be, we invite you to prayerfully consider the following:

1. **Use the tools included in this book** as part of your daily spiritual practice.
2. **Form a small group** with two or three others to walk through this book and its study guide. Or, if you have already done that—
3. **Take your group deeper** into discovering and living from your whole heart with *Wholehearted Living*, the first of our six-week small group studies. Each week includes:

- Four daily scripture reflections, plus one review day
- An overview video highlighting the week's content
- A skills video which equips you to build authentic community where it is safe to be seen and known
- A team meeting guide

For more than two decades, thousands of men and women have found a proven path to becoming wholehearted through Wellspring Group's *Battle for the Heart* and now our Wholehearted series. To discover more about Wellspring Group and how to go deeper in knowing your heart, God's heart, and the hearts of others, visit us at wellspringgroup.org/nextsteps.

Acknowledgments

To our staff who have persevered through years of stops and starts and carried extra workloads when we were holed up writing. Special thanks to Laura Arnold, who breathed life back into the book project when it faced imminent death and walked with us in the murky world of writing and publishing; and to Abby Mandella for allowing us significant chunks of time these past two years—at high cost to herself—to get this book to the finish line.

To our board, past and present, who have supported and believed in us and this book from start to finish—for over twelve years!

To our Wellspring Group donors, who have believed in the vision of being a part of inspiring a global movement of wholehearted community overflowing with the glory of God. You will never know the fullness of your reward until you see the impact in eternity.

To our many alumni, who volunteered their time and stories—reading rough drafts, giving feedback, and offering the gift of their experience in areas where we were weak or lacked knowledge. There are many more of you than we can name, but we know who you are, and we hope you hear the Father's "Well done, good and faithful servant!" for the part you played in helping us reach this milestone.

To our developmental editor, Shari Shallard, who played a significant role in helping us shape this book, and our copy editor, Lisa Stillwell, and our proofreader, Lisa Guest, who helped us polish up the final draft.

To our spouses, who persevered with us through years of writing and revising—much of which never made it into the final version. You offered encouragement, adapted your schedules to create space for us to meet deadlines, and carried extra responsibilities while we wrote. You have sacrificially loved not only us but all who will read this book.

To our God—the loving, pursuing Trinity who created us out of love, redeemed us, and is restoring us so we can more fully experience your love. We pray that in this, our offering of love, you are glorified.

Glossary of Key Terms

affirmation: see *validation*

Battle for the Heart: The internal and relational struggle of becoming a wholehearted person who reveals the glory of God. It involves choosing between the Way of Pride and the Way of Humility, and it's fought on three levels: connection to our own hearts, to God's heart, and to the hearts of others. In the context of Wellspring Group it also refers to a nine-to-ten-month spiritual formation process we offer.

choices: Decisions that flow from how we process at a conscious or subconscious level our desires, feelings, and thoughts.

desires: *Deep desires* are the deepest longings of the human heart. They flow from the image of God within us, so they can only be fully satisfied in union with the God who created us.
  Deceptive desires are surface desires we mistakenly believe will fully satisfy a deep desire.
  Surface desires are desires that are most easily identified. They can be material, positional, relational, or experiential. They are helpful in connecting us to deeper desires.

disconnect (the): The disconnect between what we think we believe and what we truly believe, often at a subconscious level, about God, ourselves, others, and life.

emotions and feelings: Emotions and feelings reveal what's going on in our hearts and bodies.
  Emotions are our body's instinctive reaction to what we experience and are largely subconscious.

Feelings are how we make sense of our emotional responses. They are shaped by our individual experiences of life and how we've historically interpreted those experiences.

Evil: Everything that exalts itself against God, including Satan, our unredeemed flesh, and the fallen world.

false visceral beliefs: Deeply held, often subconscious beliefs that contradict our biblical understanding but shape how we see God, ourselves, and others. These beliefs generally form based on how we experience our deepest desires being either met or blocked. We often react according to these beliefs in moments of pressure, sabotaging what we most long for.

fullness of life: The abundant, deeply satisfying life Jesus offers—marked by divine (God-given) intimacy, identity, and purpose.

glory (Exodus 33:18–19, 34:5–7): God's goodness, his internal essence, including his love, grace, mercy, compassion, faithfulness, and justice. In this book it is simplified to God's love, grace, and truth.

integration (of the heart): The process of recognizing and understanding how our desires, feelings, and thoughts work together, at a subconscious or conscious level, to influence what we choose. Through growing awareness, we increasingly open our whole hearts to Christ shaping our desires, identifying with and influencing our feelings, transforming our thoughts, and motivating our choices.

Larger Story: God's overarching narrative of creation, fall, redemption, and restoration.

mourning: Acknowledging and experiencing in our whole hearts the loss, damage, and pain of unmet desires. Mourning may be prompted by what has happened to us or those around us as well as from our own failures to love.

repentance: Turning from the Way of Pride by recognizing and mourning what our sin costs God, ourselves, and others; then choosing the Way of Humility and surrender to God's love.

suffering: The pain of unmet deep desires that we experience either as a result of our choices or through no fault of our own.

thoughts: Both conscious and subconscious, our thoughts include our observations, analysis, and conclusions about ourselves, others, and all of life.

validation and affirmation: Extended by an authority who has the right and the capacity to verify whatever is being considered, validation authenticates the reality or essence of something.
Affirmation recognizes what the appropriate authority has already done. Only God can validate us, but he has created human beings to echo his voice of validation.

visceral beliefs: A deep, gut-level knowing, feeling, or reaction to an experience or to ongoing experiences. Visceral beliefs about ourselves, others, God, and life form throughout life, often at a subconscious level. These beliefs powerfully affect the way we act and react in moments of pressure. When these beliefs are contrary to the biblical truth we rationally know and long to act out of, we call them *false visceral beliefs*. False visceral beliefs sabotage the fulfillment of our deepest desires.

Way of Humility: The path to becoming who you are created to be.

Way of Pride: The path that sabotages becoming who you are created to be.

wellspring of the heart: The inner source of our desires, feelings, thoughts, and choices (Proverbs 4:23 NIV 1984 edition).

wholehearted / living wholeheartedly: Living increasingly connected to your heart, God's heart, and the hearts of others.

wholehearted community: Believers in Christ coming together to experience and express God's love to him, one another, and the world.

Tools

Types of Desires

Surface Desires

Surface desires are connected to deep desires and are the most easily recognized and accessible desires.

MATERIAL

money, a new car, house, jewelry, clothes, toys

RELATIONAL

friendship, family, spouse, work

POSITIONAL

mother, father, husband, wife, particular job or title in your vocation, avocation or ministry

EXPERIENTIAL

a vacation, climb a mountain, walk in the woods, romance, sports, recreation, achievements, mother, father, husband, wife

---

Deceptive Desires

Deceptive desires are surface desires we mistakenly believe will fully satisfy a deep desire when we seek their fulfillment apart from God.

(Example: a promotion will provide a sense of significance)

Deepest Desires

Deep desires arise out of the image of God in you. They draw you to God and can only be fully satisfied through union with God.

PURPOSE

to be part of something larger, transcendence, glory

RELATIONSHIP

connection, love/be loved, pursue and be pursued, community

SECURITY

safety, to protect and provide, be protected and provided for

HONOR

respect

KNOWN & VALUED

understood, heard, seen

IMPACT

significance

DUTY

to come through, to hear "well done"

BEAUTY & CREATIVITY

to experience and create beauty

JUSTICE

for right to prevail, to see all human beings valued and respected

FREEDOM

right and capacity to freely choose

ADVENTURE

to risk for a captivating vision

PEACE & REST

wholeness, completion, home, order

JOY

pleasure, satisfaction from desires met

Feelings Chart

IDENTIFY FEELINGS WE EXPERIENCE AS POSITIVE

Peaceful	**Joyful**	**Empowered**
Comfortable	Refreshed	Strong
Secure	Stimulated	Capable
Calm	Creative	Energetic
Relaxed	Encouraged	Hopeful
Trusting	Pleased	Inspired
Safe	Happy	Respected
Protected	Full	Significant
Content	Free	Successful
Sure	Delighted	Valuable
Certain	Thrilled	Confident
Patient	Elated	Gifted
	Exhilirated	

Authentic	**Grateful**	**Loved**
Real	Satisfied	Considered
True	Sentimental	Seen
Honest	Nostalgic	Loved/Loving
Direct	Humbled	Known
Loyal	Thoughtful	Connected
Faithful	Blessed	Desirable
Aware	Thankful	Beautiful
Seen	Whole	Adored
Heard	Healed	Cherished
Known	Full	Nurtured
Glorious	Awed	Trusted
		Delighted in

IDENTIFY FEELINGS WE EXPERIENCE AS NEGATIVE

Fearful	**Sad**	**Confused**
Shy	Down	Overwhelmed
Cautious	Bored	Bewildered
Hesitant	Burdened	Torn
Insecure	Somber	Stunned
Anxious	Disappointed	Curious
Tense	Tired	Uncertain
Nervous	Dissatisfied	Ambivalent
Troubled	Discouraged	Doubtful
Distressed	Grieved	Unsettled
Scared	Depressed	Hesitant
Horrified	Defeated	Perplexed
Helpless	Empty	Puzzled
Agitated	Miserable	Distracted
Shocked	Despairing	Flustered
Alarmed	Devastated	Fragmented
Numb	Undone	Lost

Angry	**Ashamed**	**Lonely**
Hurt	Bashful	Left out
Resentful	Embarrassed	Invisible
Ticked	Awkward	Out of place
Cynical	Clumsy	Disconnected
Skeptical	Uncomfortable	Distant
Annoyed	Flustered	Excluded
Frustrated	Foolish	Isolated
Fed up	Weak	Unwanted
Indignant	Inadequate	Rejected
Jealous	Self-conscious	Despised
Disgusted	Diminished	Abandoned
Hostile	Chagrined	Desolate
Furious	Remorseful	Forsaken
Critical	Guilty	
Contemptuous	Humiliated	
Enraged	Mortified	

Elevator Model of the Heart

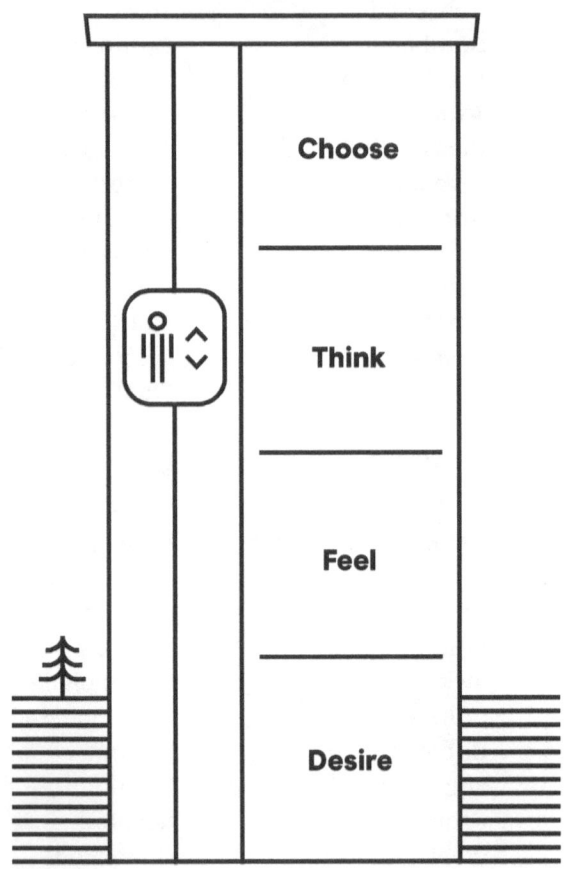

State of the Heart Template

Describe the situation:

What am I thinking?

What am I feeling?

What am I desiring?

What do I want to choose?

Engaging with Scripture from the Four Levels of the Heart

Instructions: pick one or two questions from each level. You do not need to answer all.

Thinking Level

What do I think about this passage? How does it apply to me? How have I experienced this truth? How does this seem to not match my current life experience?

Desires Level

What do I long for as I read this passage? What deep desires are being met as I receive this truth? What deep desires are not being met in places where God's truth is not yet fully realized in my life?

Feeling Level

How do I feel about this passage? How do I feel as I consider the ways I have experienced this truth? How do I feel as I struggle to reconcile this truth with my current experience of life?

Choosing

What choices do I want to make? Try to identify choices that flow from deep desires and move you toward connection with God and others. Seek to be honest about where you're struggling.

© Wellspring Group

Notes

1. Robert Waldinger, MD, and Marc Schulz, PhD, *The Good Life: Lessons from the World's Longest Scientific Study of Happiness* (New York: Simon & Schuster, 2023), 10.

2. David Benner, *Surrender to Love: Discovering the Heart of Christian Spirituality* (Lisle, IL: InterVarsity Press, 2015), 76.

3. Timothy Keller, "The Revolutionary Christian Heart," *Timothy Keller* (blog), February 6, 2015, https://timothykeller.com/blog/2015/2/6/the-revolutionary-christian-heart.

4. J. A. Thompson, *The Book of Jeremiah,* New International Commentary on the Old Testament (Grand Rapids: Eerdmans, 1980), 422.

5. Robert Saucy, *Minding the Heart* (Grand Rapids: Kregel, 2013), 86.

6. F. F. Bruce, *The Epistle to the Hebrews,* New International Commentary on the New Testament (Grand Rapids: Eerdmans, 1964), 82.

7. John Calvin, *Institutes of the Christian Religion*, trans. Henry Beveridge (Peabody, MA: Hendrickson, 2008), 13.

8. Benner, 66.

9. Ibid.

10. John H. Walton ed. *The NIV Application Commentary on the Bible: One-Volume Edition,* edited by Christopher A. Beetham and Nancy L. Erickson (Grand Rapids: Zondervan, 2024), 131.

11. John Goldingay, *Old Testament Theology: Israel's Faith*, vol. 2 (Lisle, IL: IVP Academic, 2006), 198.

12. Curt Thompson, MD, *The Soul of Desire: Discovering the Neuroscience of Longing, Beauty, and Community* (Lisle, IL: InterVarsity Press, 2021), 22.

13. Augustine, *Confessions*, trans. Henry Chadwick (Oxford: Oxford University Press, 1991), Book I, chap. 1.

14. Michael J. Wilkins, *Matthew,* The NIV Application Commentary (Grand Rapids: Zondervan Academic, 2003), 143–144.

15. R. T. France, *The Gospel of Matthew.* New International Commentary on the New Testament (Grand Rapids: Eerdmans, 2007), 127.

16 Commentary, *NIV Study Bible*, Kenneth Barker, ed. (Grand Rapids: Zondervan, 1984), p. [n.p.])

17 Douglas J. Moo, *NIV Application Commentary: 2 Peter, Jude* (Grand Rapids: Zondervan Academic, 1997), 75.

18 France, *Matthew*, 648.

19 Ibid., 1002.

20 "Captain Miller's dying words," *Saving Private Ryan*, directed by Steven Spielberg (1998; Mutual Film Company/Paramount Pictures, 1998), 2:21:00.

21 "Older James Ryan at Captain Miller's grave," *Saving Private Ryan*, 2:30:45.

22 "Older James to his wife," *Saving Private Ryan*, 2:31:30.

23 James Moffatt, *The Holy Bible Containing the Old and New Testaments: A New Translation* (Chicago: University of Chicago Press, 1922).

24 Tish Harrison Warren, *Prayer in the Night: For Those Who Work or Watch or Weep* (Lisle, IL: InterVarsity Press, 2021), 23.

25 Ibid., 26.

26 C. S. Lewis, *Mere Christianity* (New York City: Simon & Schuster, 1996), 190–191.

27 Westminster Assembly, *The Westminster Shorter Catechism* (London: 1647), Q.1.

www.ingramcontent.com/pod-product-compliance
Lightning Source LLC
LaVergne TN
LVHW041926070526
838199LV00051BA/2725